P9-DGY-376

Praise for *If the Buddha Married*

"Charlotte Kasl brings the Buddha's wisdom to the complex world of intimate relationships. In *If the Buddha Married*, she brings clarity to an area filled with confusion, and hope to an area where so many of us have far too little. We've all heard that marriage can be a spiritual experience; reading this book, you actually believe it."

—Marianne Williamson

"Charlotte Kasl once again reminds us that a love relationship is vitally alive and requires our full attention without attachment. Though filled with succinct and practical advice the curious ego will relish, the advice is immersed in spiritual wisdom that easily moves the reader to the heart where love dwells."

—Brenda M. Schaeffer, author of *Is It Love or Is It Addiction?* and *Love's Way*

"Charlotte Kasl has skillfully integrated Buddhist spiritual concepts with her many years of clinical experience in treating those couples who seek to improve their love relationships. *If the Buddha Married*'s greatest contribution lies in the specific examples of good interactions and problem ones, plus ways of resolving them. Her book will increase the mutual understanding of many couples."

—John and Helen Watkins, authors of *Ego States: Theory and Therapy*

Praise for *If the Buddha Dated*

"Insightful, clear, humorous, delightful . . . A must-read for all people who value honesty, kindness, and compassion in the affairs of the heart.

—Susan Page, author of *If I'm So Wonderful, Why Am I Still Single?*

Compass
If THE BUDDHA MARRIED

Charlotte Sophia Kasl, Ph.D., formerly a professional pianist, has been a practicing psychotherapist and workshop leader for over twenty-five years. She has a longtime involvement with social activism, feminism, Reiki healing, Eastern spiritual practices, the Society of Friends, and alternative healing. She has written extensively on addiction, relationships, sexuality, and healing, weaving together many aspects of spirituality and psychology to bring a holistic, empowering approach to all her work. Her books include *If the Buddha Dated*; *Finding Joy*; *Many Roads, One Journey*; *Women, Sex and Addiction*; *A Home for the Heart*; and *Yes, You Can! A Guide to Empowerment Groups*. Formerly of Minneapolis, Minnesota, she now lives in an octagonal house on a mountain near Missoula, Montana, where she writes and has a psychotherapy practice.

OTHER BOOKS BY CHARLOTTE KASL

If the Buddha Dated: A Handbook for Finding Love on a Spiritual Path

A Home for the Heart: Creating Intimacy and Community with Loved Ones, Neighbors, and Friends

Finding Joy: 101 Ways to Free Your Spirit and Dance with Life

Yes, You Can! A Guide to Empowerment Groups

Many Roads, One Journey: Moving Beyond the Twelve Steps

Women, Sex, and Addiction: A Search for Love and Power

CHARLOTTE SOPHIA KASL, PH.D.

IF THE BUDDHA MARRIED

*Creating Enduring Relationships
on a Spiritual Path*

Penguin Compass

PENGUIN BOOKS

Published by the Penguin Group

Penguin Putnam Inc., 375 Hudson Street, New York, New York 10014, U.S.A.

Penguin Books Ltd, 80 Strand, London WC2R 0RL, England

Penguin Books Australia Ltd, 250 Camberwell Road,
Camberwell, Victoria 3124, Australia

Penguin Books Canada Ltd, 10 Alcorn Avenue, Toronto, Ontario, Canada M4V 3B2

Penguin Books India (P) Ltd, 11 Community Centre,
Panchsheel Park, New Delhi – 110 017, India

Penguin Books (N.Z.) Ltd, Cnr Rosedale and Airborne Roads,
Albany, Auckland, New Zealand

Penguin Books (South Africa) (Pty) Ltd, 24 Sturdee Avenue,
Rosebank, Johannesburg 2196, South Africa

Penguin Books Ltd, Registered Offices: Harmondsworth, Middlesex, England

First published in Penguin Compass 2001

5   7   9   10   8   6   4

Grateful acknowledgment is made for permission
to reprint selections from the following copyrighted works:
The Essential Rumi, translations by Coleman Barks with John Moyne.
By permission of the publisher, Threshold Books.
Like This by Rumi, versions by Coleman Barks, Maypop Books.
© Coleman Barks, 1990. By permission of Coleman Barks.
The Prophet by Kahil Gibran. Copyright 1923 by Kahil Gibran and renewed
1951 by Administrators C.T.A. of Kahil Gibran Estate and Mary G. Gibran.
Reprinted by premission of Alfred A. Knopf, a division of Random House, Inc.

CIP data available

ISBN 0 14 01.9622 6

Printed in the United States of America
Set in Goudy
Designed by Sabrina Bowers

Dedicated to
John and Helen Watkins
. . . And all people seeking to bring love, peace, and justice
into their lives and into the world

HEARTFELT THANKS TO . . .

Janet Goldstein, my editor of ten years, for enthusiasm, detailed suggestions, and helping shape this book.

Susan Hans O'Connor, for general feedback and intrepid courage in making cuts.

Blake dePastino, who went over the complete manuscript, and spent several days at my house helping to rearrange chapters, edit, and provide encouragement and stability in the midst of troubled computers and general angst.

As always, a bouquet of roses to Edite Kroll, my agent of fourteen years, for friendship, support, advice, and humor. Hot tea and lunch to Judi Kolenda, who has been my office assistant, and anchor, throughout the writing of this book

And many thanks to all the people who contributed in one form or another by teaching me, telling their stories, and giving input and suggestions. I am always astounded by the openness and willingness of so many people to talk about their lives. I am humbled by the wisdom and insight that they so generously gave so that others may learn: Stephen Wolinsky, Sigurd Hoppe, Suzie Risho, Lindsay Richards and Tom Roberts, Dodie and Roger Moquin, Bob and Grace Lucas, Judy Stevens, Don and Mary Nelson, Helen and John Watkins, Lizzie Juda and Steve Nelson, Vicki and Tim Mathews, Stu and Marvel Stewart, Martha Boesing, Pat Bik,

Jeanine Walker, Tammie Milligan, Lynette Christensen, Kyoko Katayama and Eric Stull, and Judith Reynolds. And for just being there with humor, tenderness, and love, thanks to Zamilla, Leslie Ojala, Jody Marshall, Starshine, the Sufi community of the Missoula area, and members of the Missoula Friends Meeting. I also want to acknowledge the mountains, rivers, rocks, hiking trails, and pine trees that form this beautiful landscape that surrounds me and lifts up my heart on a daily basis.

Also, to the next generation, best wishes for creating enduring, loving relationships: Janel and Rodney, Lawrence and Kim, Alex and Tony, Kathy and Rob.

Bright blessing to you all.

CONTENTS

PART III
Look in Your Own Mirror

PART IV
The Daily Practice of Living and Loving

PART V
When I Was a Child, I Spoke as a Child:
Am I Still Doing It Now?

PART VI
Communion Is the Purpose of Communication

PART VII
Make Friends with Conflict

INTRODUCTION

The river that flows in you also flows in me.
—Kabir

There *are* couples who sustain warm, vital relationships for many years. Many of them remain romantically and sexually attracted to each other as their connection becomes deeper and richer.

This book is about creating a loving, trusting bond with a special partner—a bond based on a deep level of knowing, understanding, and compassion that allows each person to flow easily between separateness and oneness. It shows how vitality, spontaneity, and freedom emerge as we become able to see our partner clearly—free from images, illusions, and expectations.

From a Buddhist perspective, the spiritual path of awakening includes understanding our attachments—how our expectations, fears, and demands lie at the root of our individual suffering, including our suffering in relationships. We learn to bring awareness to our own behavior, including our intense reactions to our partner's words or actions. We discover how we can use our highly charged flashes of emotion to help us wake up rather than retreat from our relationships. We learn to stay present to ourselves and acknowledge our anger, fear, or hurt, so we cease hiding from ourselves and those we love. This in turn opens us to the possibility of an intimate, lively, enduring relationship.

As we loosen our tenacious hold on behaviors and beliefs that keep us acting and reacting in predictable, unconscious ways, we begin to glimpse the freedom of an open mind, sometimes known in spiritual teachings as Zen mind or "beginner's mind." We begin to see into the heart of each other with understanding, kindness, and care, and an awareness that transcends words. Fascination, humor, and delight replace fear, clinging, and worry. With a "beginner's mind," we are able to live in the present. We see ourselves and our beloved afresh each day, as we learn to dance lightly with one another amidst life's unfolding dramas. We stay alive to each other through an ongoing process of asking questions: Who are you? Who am I? What do *you* feel, need, think, and want? What do *I* feel, need, think, and want? Thus, our relationship becomes dynamic and alive rather than static and predictable.

This book does not offer the concept of a perfect marriage, although I include stories of people who have had extremely successful, long-term, nurturing relationships. Rather, it encourages people to immerse themselves in the current of the river that flows through life and meet the shifting rapids, logjams, and clear waters with fascination and interest. It shows how our individual spiritual journey and our emotional development are deeply entwined with our ability to create an intimate union with another.

There is no one path for all couples to follow and no stereotype that predicts success. The people I have interviewed for this book reflected immense differences. One couple met on their first day of college and have been together ever since. Others had numerous tumultuous or empty relationships before creating one that worked. For some, it was a first marriage; for others, it was a second or even a third. Some had large age differences; in two cases, the woman was fourteen years older than her husband. There were also variations in race, religion, sexual affinity, spiritual beliefs, class, and cultural backgrounds. But the health of their relationships had far more to do with self-awareness, commitment, openness, acceptance, shared values, and the ability to embrace differences and handle conflict—along with a strong attraction and liking for each other—than with the length of their courtship or the details of their personal history.

Because differences are inevitable in relationships, we will explore how to handle the conflicts that naturally arise when our differences meet, along with the ways we unconsciously create fights to keep us apart, create excitement, or release tension. Readers can learn to become more conscious of the sources of conflict as they recognize the old hardwired "fight and flight" responses that echo their childhood—the angry adolescent saying, "Don't tell me what to do," or a frightened child pleading, "Please tell me that you love me." We can learn to come into the present so we are not controlled by these age-old reactions.

Dealing skillfully with conflict will not always result in complete resolution. But by bringing goodwill and maintaining a broad perspective, differences can exist comfortably within a loving bond. As one couple told me, "It's not that issues don't keep coming up, or that we always find solutions, it's that we have the security and confidence to sit down and discuss any conflict, knowing that we will be heard and listened to, knowing that it will not pull us apart."

If the Buddha Married explores ways to come alive and be authentic, as opposed to creating a patchwork quilt that holds the relationship together but obscures the possibility of true connection. It does not focus on superficial Band-Aids for relationships—to be nicer, more mysterious, to give more compliments—or other recipes for behavior that create a false persona. Rather, it helps people reach deep inside so they are aware of whatever hinders them from being open, accepting, and loving toward their partner in a heartfelt way. We can apply this to all our relationships throughout our lives.

This book underscores how a commitment to knowing and accepting oneself and one's partner helps create a context of trust and safety. As we learn to live in the present, free of old images and expectations, each person feels safe to voice their thoughts and feelings, and express love. This in turn nurtures the experience of "us," the special realm of union and connection that provides a shelter for the couple and allows each individual to be more than he or she could be alone.

This journey toward intimacy and union asks us to approach the protected ground of buried hurts and fears that inevitably appears when we open ourselves completely to another. For whatever we disown within us will be reflected in the distance we keep from others. The willingness to crack the armor around our hearts is often set in motion by a yearning to experience a love that is deeper, richer, sweeter, riper, and more connected. For all of us, the spiritual journey requires a willingness to step repeatedly into the uncharted territory of each new day and our ever-changing partner. Ultimately, a Buddha marriage becomes a deep experience of joining together: we attune to both ourselves and our partner through words, gestures, looks, touches, and silence. It is a connection woven of moment-to-moment awareness. In the words of the ecstatic poet Kabir, we remember that "the river that flows in you also flows in me." This river of life is always there, pulsing within us and between us. We just need to step beyond our egos, judgments, and fears so we can experience it.

For the intrepid travelers who are willing to meet both their fears and their passions, the rewards are many—an increased ease, trust, joy, clarity, and ability to handle conflict, along with a more enduring, vital, passionate, sexual bond that will continue to flow like a clear stream in spring.

PART ONE

THE SPIRITUAL PATH
TO LOVE

1 BUDDHISM FOR LOVERS AND PARTNERS

May all beings everywhere be free from suffering and
the root of all suffering.
May all beings everywhere find happiness and the
root of all happiness.

—*Buddhist blessing*

Buddhist teachings provide a wonderful foundation to understand why relationships work and why they don't. They help us develop awareness so we live in the present and become alive to ourselves and our loved ones. Our exploration of vital, loving relationships will include Buddhist concepts of impermanence, lovingkindness, compassion, attachments, the nature of our conditioned responses, and the underlying unity of All That Is.

Buddhist teachings apply to everyday living as well as intimate relationships. Indeed, there is no separation between the awareness of how we breathe, think, talk, eat, walk, rest, work, play and the awareness of how we relate to others and to all sentient life. As we learn to bring attention to whatever we are doing, we find that all of life is a form of meditation. There is simply the experience of the moment, and our task on the spiritual path is to be engaged fully in whatever is happening right now, without judgment or expectations.

We come to realize that happiness, pain, sadness, and joy are the passing winds of our ever-changing experience, closely aligned with our identification with our mind and thoughts. As

4 ㉖ If the Buddha Married

our mind becomes quieter, we are more able to attune to the present moment, which allows us to see into the heart of things. We come to accept that for everyone, life is unpredictable, difficult, and wondrous. This, in turn, allows us to cherish, forgive, and love our brothers and sisters on this imperfect human path.

When the prince Siddhartha Gautama became known as The Buddha, meaning "the enlightened one," he had spent five years being intentionally celibate. Before he left the palace of his father and mother, however, to find a solution to the universal suffering of humankind, he was married to a beautiful princess and was the father of one son. So, we are faced with the paradox that prior to enlightenment, Buddha was married, and when he began his spiritual search for the causes of suffering, he became celibate. One might rightly ask, then, why would we look for wisdom on marriage from a man who left his wife and child for a life of celibacy? The answer lies in his exploration into the roots of human suffering and the profound wisdom of his teachings that lead to joy, compassion, and loving kindness—traits that free us to form loving relationships.

Buddhism is more about experience than beliefs. There is no concept of a supreme God—no father, mother, or unseen being out there, guiding us, controlling us, comforting us, or giving us a hand to hold. There is also no one judging us, or telling us we are right or wrong. Rather, we take refuge in the teachings, and the support of our community of like-minded brothers and sisters. We gauge the clarity and goodness of our actions through attunement to our heart and mind, asking if we are being guided by kindness and compassion in all things. As a couple, we are full and equal partners on the path of awakening, joining together, learning from each other, yet each on our own journey. Buddhism embraces the belief that all life is sacred and interconnected. That underneath our surface behaviors and thoughts lies the essence of our being, a unifying force that flows through all of us.

Buddhism has no concept of sin Rather it embraces the belief that we harm others out of our own unconsciousness or ignorance. If we were fully awake we would experience that to harm another is to harm ourselves, and that to harm ourselves is to harm another. There is no separation. As we come to fully understand this, we become less reactive to others and respond without fear or malice in our hearts.

Here is an overview of some basic Buddhist principles that are central to loving relationships.

1. *Emptiness is form, form is emptiness: we are all connected.*

This concept, which lies at the heart of Buddhism, asserts that everything is made of emptiness. Said another way, there is a unifying energy that underlies all life. At our deepest level, we are essence—the universal I Am. But we also live in a physical body and have a set of beliefs, values, and expectations that we have adopted. Unfortunately, we often identify with these beliefs to the exclusion of experiencing our essential nature, which some people may call Source, God, Spirit, All That Is, or Essence. To be at peace with ourselves and to create intimacy, we need to connect with our deepest essence and realize we existed prior to all these learned thoughts, habits, and beliefs we adopted. If we peel back the thoughts and perceptions we have learned and try to find something solid to identify with that is uniquely who we are, something that goes beyond conditioning, we find that everything dissolves and we drop into essence. There is simply nothing solid we can adhere to that defines who we are. This is both frightening and freeing—frightening to our mind and ego, freeing to our heart, which wants to experience love.

Paradoxically, it is through this emptiness that we find our wholeness and experience love, because there is nothing in the way. We are completely unified.

We can extend this idea of unity to everything in our daily lives. In his commentaries on *The Heart of Understanding*, Thich Nhat Hanh writes, "Everything contains everything else." He uses the phrase "inter-are." We are the clouds, the water, the forest, the earth that is contained in the food we eat, the air we breathe, the water we drink. We also are permeated by the vibration of our partner's touch, voice, laughter, kisses, smiles, and frowns. Everything becomes a form of energy, moving and shifting within us and between us. It is only an illusion that we are separate. As we become conscious of the deep level of "interbeing" with our partner and all people, we become exquisitely aware of the importance of being mindful of our behavior and words.

2. *Using the four noble truths to create awareness.*

At the foundation of Buddha's teachings are the four noble truths. They show how we create our own suffering through our attachments, expectations, and demands that people and situations be different than they are. By examining our attachments, we see the numerous ways in which we try to control others instead of accepting them as they are.

The first noble truth is that suffering is inherent to life. The second noble truth asserts that we suffer because of our attachments—our craving, clinging, and demanding. The third noble truth is that Nirvana—equanimity, peace, and cessation of craving—is possible and available to all when we cease our attachments. The fourth noble truth is that there is an eightfold path that leads to being free of attachments. They often are called the signposts to being on the path. They include Right Understanding, Right Aspiration, Right Action, Right Speech, Right Livelihood, Right Effort, Right Concentration, and Right Mindfulness. I would add the signpost of right relationships.

I first came into contact with the concept that I create my own suffering through my attachments in 1980 at the Cornucopia Center founded by Ken Keyes, author of *Handbook to Higher Consciousness*. It was perhaps the greatest single awakening of my life. I learned that when someone yelled at me or appeared not to like me, it meant they were attached to my being different, not that I was bad. Similarly, I discovered that when I felt impatient or angry, this reflected my attachment to someone behaving differently. *I learned that my conditioning and expectations created my turmoil, not the words or actions of the other person.*

The belief that we do harm out of ignorance doesn't take away our responsibility for our actions, but it suggests that we might better explore the pain or needs beneath our behavior rather than judging ourselves harshly or sinking into shame. This awareness was key to changing my relationships because it removed all levels of blame and shame, and helped me to realize that everyone is just doing what they are conditioned to do. Though I felt greatly relieved to understand this teaching, I did not instantly stop feeling hurt, angry, or sad. However, more and more often, I could interrupt my habituated responses by stepping back and witnessing that my reactions stemmed from *my* attachments. It was like creating a pause that allowed my mind to switch gears. Needless to say, becoming aware of attachments takes daily practice.

To love better and feel more openhearted and unified with others, start to notice your attachments to thoughts and behavior of yourself and your partner. Whenever you are agitated, upset, angry, mad, or hurt, you have an attachment to something being different than it is or you are afraid of the outcome. You are resisting the "what is" of the moment. As you observe your experience and all the accompanying feelings, realize you are creating your emotional state.

In relationships, people become attached to praise, validation, sex, security, status, and affirmations of their worth. Sentiments like "You *make* me feel so bad" or "You *make* me feel so good" are both forms of attachment because no one can *make* us feel secure and our partner is not here to tell us we're okay. This doesn't mean that loving couples don't validate or give support to each other, it's that they don't depend on it from their partner. It is given as a natural outpouring of love and care.

As we loosen our attachments, our mind starts to quiet down and we feel more attuned to others. Our attachments don't disappear, but we see them for what they are—the chattering of our conditioned mind. When we step back and ask, "Now what am I demanding that's making me so upset?" we become a witness to the unfolding drama of our lives. We start to see it as a passing show. We are in it, but not of it.

A word of caution: Some people hide behind the concept of attachment to stay in a harmful relationship. They rationalize abuse by saying, "I'm just attached to his being different." This masks the deeper attachment, namely, that the person is staying in a painful relationship for security, or because they fear being alone. So, remember, take these teachings in spirit and use them to create greater happiness in your life, not to hide.

It's a habit of yours to walk slowly
You hold a grudge for years
With such heaviness, how can you be modest?
With such attachments, do you expect to arrive anywhere?
　　　　　　　　　　　　　　—Rumi, "Bismillah"

3. *Experience lovingkindness.*

My religion is kindness.
     —Dalai Lama

Wishing: in gladness and in safety,
     May all beings be at ease . . .
Let none, through anger of ill-will
     Wish harm upon another.
     So with a boundless heart
Should one cherish all living beings.
     —Buddha

Can you gaze at your beloved and completely wish him freedom from suffering and the root of all suffering? Can you look at your partner, and with all your heart wish her the fullness of all that she can become? Do your actions and words reflect these loving wishes? When two people fully open their hearts, wanting only the best for each other, they ease through the boundaries of their separateness. This is the essence of lovingkindness.

The foundation of lovingkindness is bringing an unconditional friendliness and acceptance to ourselves. We realize that everything is part of our Buddha nature and there is nothing to reject. Kahlil Gibran writes in *The Prophet*, "In our giant self lies our goodness, and that goodness is in all of us. Lovingkindness is like bringing a vast embrace to all we are and feeling the radiance at the center of our being."

From this place of self-acceptance and expansiveness, we feel steady, natural, and unafraid. When lovingkindness permeates our being, we are so transparent and at ease within ourselves that anger and hostility have no place to take root inside. Once we have experienced the wonderful expansiveness of lovingkindness, we become highly attuned to the constricting nature of holding on to grief, anger, hurt, or loss.

One step toward experiencing lovingkindness comes from immersing ourselves in our own lives, following our heart and giving ourselves fully to whatever we feel called to do. This allows us to cheer completely for others as they come into their power and find their path. If we stand in the shadows of our own lives, shrinking from the vast possibilities before us, we are likely to be jealous or uncomfortable around people who fully explore their own potential.

Lovingkindness does not mean we fake a smile or do not protect ourselves. Sharon Salzberg, in her wonderful book, *Lovingkindness*, tells a story of a woman who was riding in an open rickshaw when she was suddenly attacked by two people trying to steal her purse. She later asked a spiritual teacher what he would have done. He said something to the effect of With lovingkindness, I would have taken my umbrella and whacked them on the head. We can say no with lovingkindness, we can end a relationship with lovingkindness. It's simply that we see people doing what they are conditioned to do, and at the same time we take care of ourselves.

Experiencing joy also brings us to lovingkindness. Joy is like an effervescence of the heart bursting open with awe, wonder, and a big smile at the predicament of living. Many people are more comfortable bonding in pain and sadness than coming together in delight and pleasure. Joy is a powerful energy that sweeps through our bodies, breaking up tension, exposing our wounded places, and expanding our ability to embrace all feelings. The freer our energy, the more spacious we feel inside.

When we stop making a big deal out of our inner experience

by either running from it or dramatizing it, we start feeling lighter about these human traits. As a result, we feel our commonalities with others—"I know where that comes from: I've done that. I've stolen, I've fudged on the truth, been afraid, or arrogant." This allows us to be present to the pain of another, just to be right there, doing nothing but providing a safe space for our partner to feel. From this silent yet alive place, we will start to feel more connected to ourselves and our beloved.

4. *Accept the impermanence of life.*

We have no fixed self—every aspect of our being is in constant motion. From health to jobs, to interests to friendships, to sexual desire to the weather—everything is constantly decaying, regenerating, and in flux. It follows, then, that relationships are not fixed. A couple comes for therapy wanting sex to be hot, just as it was when they first took that flight on gossamer wings. But that exact moment is gone; it will never come again. Our needs, wants, feelings, thoughts, moods, and desires are constantly shifting, so our relationships are always changing, too. Life is a river of loss, change, and rebirth.

By accepting impermanence, we realize that relationships become a dance of resonating in the moment with our partner as well as ourself—from our thoughts and feelings, to our changing bodies, to the look in our lover's eyes. As we let go of fixed perceptions and expectations we start to experience the amazing expansiveness and lightheartedness that comes from living in the present moment. We stop saying things such as "But you used to like it that way" or "We've always done it that way." Instead, "Who are you now?" is the question we bring to every day.

When we truly accept impermanence and the daily losses that are inevitable, we may feel a thread of grief running through our

life. In Buddhist temples, there is often a bouquet of flowers to remind us that nothing stays the same. But if we can watch the
flowers and see them as moving through a cycle—they will soon
be part of the compost heap that will become part of other plants
and flowers—then we free our mind to be one with the continuity
of life.

5. *Recognize samsara, the wheel of suffering.*

> *As long as you stay unconscious, asleep at the switch of your
> own life, true happiness will prove elusive.*
> —*Lama Surya Das,* AWAKENING THE BUDDHA WITHIN

She says, "I don't want to talk right now," and her partner feels
a familiar wave of pain. He says, "I'll be seeing a friend on Saturday afternoon," and his partner is instantly jealous. She asks for
help around the house, and her partner responds, "You always
boss me around," or, worse, says, "Yeah, sure," and does nothing.
Many couples have arguments about time, money, sex, activities,
or children that are so predictable they could probably write the
script in advance.

To be free, happy, and live from our essence, we need to explore our conditioned responses, known as "samsara," which
"keep us asleep at the switch of our own lives." Samsara is about
the suffering inherent in living a shallow existence of habituated
patterns without reflection, contemplation, or understanding. It is
the suffering of not being fully alive and awake. It's as if our life is
happening, but we're not there. In relationships, we act and react
to our partner in the same ways, over and over again, dulling the
spark and putting the relationship to sleep.

To increase the intimacy in your life, start noticing the pre-

dictable ways in which you act and react in relation to your partner. Notice if you dominate the conversation or shrink with fear.
Notice if you are truly taking the needs of your partner to heart.
Notice the excuses you make to avoid sex. Notice the complaints,
theories, or points you have attempted to make a hundred times.
To bring more vitality to your relationship and loosen the entrenched patterns, stop acting in the same predictable ways. Do
something different. Anything! When the same old conversation
starts rolling down the track, you can say, "We've already had this
conversation. Let's do something different."

It can help to look underneath the predictable behavior for
deeper levels of truth, which, if brought to the surface, would
bring life back to the relationship: "I'm making excuses to not
have sex, because it seems so mechanical and I'm not enjoying
it." "I go to Jim's on Saturday because you always expect me to
work all day around the house, and I want to have some fun."
"I'm terrified to look at our money situation because I feel so out
of control with my spending." When we get closer to the bones of
truth, we get closer to each other, and open the possibility of
something new happening.

We may not know consciously how separate and distant we
are, but we experience it physically, emotionally, and in our inability to experience wonder, delight, and happiness. Habituated
patterns create distance because we are self-absorbed and unconscious; openness and truth bring us closer together because we are
awake and able to look into the eyes of our beloved. You can start
noticing different degrees of closeness and separateness in your
body, even in tiny degrees of difference. Distance often feels dry,
dull, boring, or lonely. Closeness usually brings warmth, lightness,
joy, and a sense of peace.

Sometimes, we feel at a loss to act or react in new ways even if we want to. That's where exploring samsara leads to a natural meeting of Buddhism and psychology. From a psychological perspective, our conditioned responses—compulsions, fear, anger, hurt, or shame—are hardwired in our brain and attached to the nervous system. They often go off automatically in spite of our strongest wishes to the contrary.

Not all of our habituated responses are about past trauma. It is often the nature of life to have conflicting pulls between inertia and taking action, between awareness and unconsciousness. We want to watch TV all day and have a clean house. We want to eat Twinkies but still be thin. We want to have a close relationship but not reveal our fears or take time for each other. This calls for us to exert ourselves and push through inertia. As always on the path, staying awake takes a daily commitment to tune in to ourselves, reach deeper, and speak from our heart.

Essentially, the Buddhist path is one of waking up—opening our minds, taking off our armor, and finding that tender spot in our hearts. Everything can be a vehicle for waking up—a wonderful lover, a heated argument, dead batteries, sickness, success, whatever is happening in the moment. We can either accept our experience and wake up, or we can go to sleep by dozing off and resisting our experience. Ultimately, we let go of all teachings and accept the motion of life in the moment—vital, dynamic, changing. The end point is letting go of all of it and simply being present in life, with a loving heart and a free mind.

2 SAY HELLO TO YOUR BELOVED: SUFISM

Fill your cup, drink it up
The fish in the water's not thirsty
    —*From* THE DANCES OF UNIVERSAL PEACE

While the principles in this book center around Buddhism, I also draw on aspects of Sufism and Quaker practice, which I will explain briefly here. Sufism is often called "the path of the heart." It is not so much about the idea that God is love, rather that God is found in the loving between one another. To love one person is to love all, and to love all is to love each individual. If Buddhism is about meeting the emptiness and feeling at one with the void, Sufism is more about filling oneself up and surrendering to the ecstasy of nature, love, and being one with All That Is. There is an ecstatic quality to a good relationship—a joy beyond words amidst life's daily rituals and tasks, a joy of being one with our beloved.

Sufis greet each other as Beloved, or Beloved sister or Beloved brother. This reminds us that we all reside in the heart of God, in the heart of the Beloved that is the underlying essence of All That Is. The first time someone greeted me as Beloved Charlotte at a Sufi gathering, tears came to my eyes, and my heart melted. To this day, when I receive an e-mail addressed to "Beloved Sister Rhamana" (my Sufi name), or someone greets me as Beloved, a warmth and sweetness penetrate my heart. Recently, when a Sufi friend and I were planning a dinner and talking about how much ice cream to buy, she said with a smile, "Not too much. These are our Beloveds and ice cream isn't very good for us." In other words, everyone known or unknown is our Beloved and we extend our loving care to all. For me, thinking of everyone as Beloved is parallel to Buddhism's concept of lovingkindness.

Take a moment to think of your partner (or a special friend) as your beloved. Take a deep breath, relax your belly, and let the meaning of the word drench your heart—this special person who wants what you want—to be loved, to be free of suffering, and to experience joy. This imperfect being who has chosen you as you have chosen him or her. This one whose touch, voice, habits, and smells are embedded in your senses. This one who shares the journey with you for better or worse.

Think of a love within you so rich and flowing that it can dissolve whatever is hard or knotted or afraid in your heart. Imagine a free-flowing energy so vast it spills out of you and into the heart of your beloved, taking you both to that place beneath illusions where there is nothing but love.

Don't say God is in your heart
Say, You are in the Heart of God.
  —*Kahlil Gibran,* THE PROPHET

3   LEARN TO TRUST YOURSELF: THE SOCIETY OF FRIENDS

Dearly Beloved Friends, these things we do not lay upon you as a rule or form to walk by; but that all, with a measure of the light, which is pure and holy, may be guided: and so in the light walking and abiding, these things may be fulfilled in the Spirit, not in the letter; for the letter killeth but the Spirit giveth life.

> —Postscript to an epistle to "the brethren
>   in the north" issued by a meeting of elders
>   at Balby, Yorkshire, England, 1656

Quakers draw on a wide range of teachings and literature, but believe that discerning our truths as they arise, and living by them, is at the heart of the spiritual journey. Silent reflection is the means to hearing the guidance that emanates from that still, small voice within. This deep level of listening allows people to speak simply and clearly from the heart—a quality of profound importance to loving relationships. Like Buddhism, Quaker practice is not so much about beliefs as the ways we live—threading silence, kindness, and awareness through our days, being mindful of our actions and our effect on others.

Quakers value group unity, but not at the exclusion of each member being true to her- or himself. It's as if we have two threads winding through us simultaneously—our individual perspective, and our commitment to maintaining unity for the greatest good of the group. Translated to relationships, this becomes the balance between "I," "you," and "us"—a balance that was always evident with successful couples I interviewed, no matter what their religious beliefs or nonbeliefs.

Quakers don't use the term "church"; rather, we gather for meeting for worship. The place is inconsequential because Quakers use no objects or symbols or sacred texts. Couples married in the Quaker tradition are considered "under the care of the meeting." This means the Quaker meeting is committed to being supportive and available. Buddhism talks about taking refuge in the *sangha*—the community of others on the spiritual path. Likewise, couples need a supportive community for their life as a couple.

Quakers make decisions by consensus—a process I have taught to many couples. Consensus does not mean that individuals wholeheartedly agree in all things. It's that they come to decisions based on a process of listening, understanding, and speaking their mind as they seek a positive solution that is agreeable for all concerned. This prevents people from winning and losing, which inevitably leads to resentments, anger, feelings of alienation, or being considered unimportant. Reaching consensus may seem laborious on occasion, but through the process, couples come to experience the deep satisfaction of belonging to and valuing their relationship. It is truly an exercise in stepping beyond the ego, reaching for the truth and seeking the highest good for the group or couple.

Quakers apply the concept of simplicity to words, possessions, and lifestyle also. This simplicity is not about austerity, but rather about having just enough, but not more than we need. This helps create time for what is important—namely, introspection, pursuing our interests, connecting with the people we love, and being of service in the world.

What binds Buddhism, Sufism, and Quaker practices together is a belief in our interconnectedness; profound respect for others; being guided by a greater good beyond material possessions, status, and image; valuing silence and stillness of the mind; acceptance of differences; developing inner awareness of one's perceptions and motivation; commitment to service; and seeking guidance from within. While the successful couples I interviewed were of different faiths, religions, and cultural backgrounds, they had found their way to these universal principles, either in part or in whole.

4   EXPLORE THE SOURCE OF AN ENDURING BOND

Happy couples drink each other in. The healthy union grants its partners liberation from the confines of the self, release from the prison of ego. . . . When we become part of something larger than ourselves, we can be released from the need to worry constantly about our own needs and failings.

—*Catherine Johnson,* LUCKY IN LOVE

I recently met an author friend, Sara, and her husband, Ed, walking up Blue Mountain near Missoula on a crisp fall day. In the ensuing conversation about writing, I mentioned this book, and I asked them if they had any wisdom to share on the success of their thirty-six-year marriage. They had survived, and even seemed to thrive, through the usual passages of child-rearing, moves, changing careers, and coauthorship of a book. Sara laughed and glanced at Ed, who grinned back. She quipped, "Stubborn. We're stubborn!" When I asked her to say more, she responded: "It means you don't bail out when it gets tough. You have long-term thinking for a long-term relationship. You really mean it when you make a commitment."

Their response was echoed by many couples I interviewed. "I just wouldn't get divorced, no matter what," one partner said. "I get mad at him, but I would miss him so much," said another. "I can't imagine being without her." Enduring couples do not boast perfection, rather they have forged an enduring bond that enriches their lives as they navigate through the great big messy journey called life.

Some of the fundamental traits that typified the couples with successful long-term relationships included:

1. A strong liking/attraction to each other, often from the moment they met; many said they were best friends.
2. A deep level of commitment to being a couple as well as separate individuals.
3. An ability to resolve conflict.
4. Shared values, dreams, and lifestyle.
5. Showing appreciation, respect, care, and consideration for each other.
6. Taking pleasure and delight in each other's company.
7. A capacity to pull together during hard times.
8. Strong connections to community and a commitment to being of service to others.

9. A good sense of humor and an ability to laugh at and reflect on themselves.
10. Supporting each other to be their best self.

Let's look at the concept of an enduring relationship by first considering what endurance means.

> *Definitions of endurance: continuation, continuity, dura-*
> *tion, persistence*
> *Synonyms: tolerance, stamina, toleration*
> *Related: fortitude, grit, guts, strength, vigor, patience, suf-*
> *ferance, steadfastness, steadiness, opposition, resis-*
> *tance*

I don't want to give the impression that relationships are solely about stamina and persistence. Marriage, whether it's legal or understood, is also about delight, pleasure, shared activities, and friendship. Yet all the couples I interviewed who have maintained vital, lasting relationships showed many traits of endurance. Here are a few:

TOLERANCE

Successful couples become adept at accepting different styles in their partners. In interviews, they were quick to identify diverging values and habits. When I asked Charles and Liz, happily married for forty-six years, about their differences, he said, smiling at Liz, "I have more expensive tastes—I like to eat out at nice restaurants, or buy a new car, or have expensive hunting dogs, but she'd rather give the money to a homeless shelter or help our kids." Liz rejoined, looking at him fondly, "Well, that's true, it definitely comes up. I'm more conservative that way." Charles went on: "I like to play the stereo and she likes it quiet, so if I go out of the room for fifteen minutes she turns it off." Again Liz smiled sheepishly, as if revealing a secret: "Yes, I do that. I can't read or concentrate with the music on. Charles can do anything with the music playing."

What set their discussion apart from less satisfied couples were the knowing looks, laughter, and lack of defensiveness. For forty years, you turn the music up, and I turn it down. It was simply: "This is how we're different." It was taken at face value without adding layers of meaning and interpretations that are typical of troubled couples: "You don't respect me, you don't care about me, if you loved me, you'd . . ."

Enduring couples understand that they both come as a package deal and they accept differences. In another situation, Kenneth and Margaret were nearing their fiftieth year of marriage when I joined them for a Quaker gathering at a friend's home. When we were leaving, Kenneth quietly said good-bye to the hosts and went to their car. I followed him as Margaret continued chatting, making the rounds of everyone who had attended. After ten minutes passed, I asked Kenneth, "Should I go in and tell her we're out here?" "Oh, no," he said, with a droll smile. "I gave that up *long* ago."

In an interview with a group of married women, when we discussed sexuality, one woman commented, referring to her husband, "Well, you know Jim, he likes guidebooks for everything—carpentry, plumbing, gardening—so he bought one of those how-to-do-it sex books. I just laughed and said, 'That's not what sex is about for me, it's about you and me, how we love each other. . . .' But it made me laugh. It was so like him."

If there was a theme to these stories, it was a fond "That's just the way she/he is." Repeatedly, happy couples were able to observe and cherish each other's differences and foibles, even when they created an inconvenience.

This brings to mind the Buddhist phrase "Abandon hope": Abandon hope of changing some of the little things in your partner. Abandon hope that your partner will start being on time, will learn to cook better, will be less scattered, will lose fifteen pounds, or balance the checkbook more accurately. Ask yourself, How would our lives be if I just accepted her or him the way she or he is? What if now and forever I quit harping, making subtle suggestions, or casually leaving clippings on the breakfast table to prove my point? Maggie applied this principle to her lover, who was routinely late for their Saturday-afternoon hike.

"The last time, when I started to feel irritated, I thought, 'Oh, I don't want to get caught in anger.' Then the phrase 'Abandon hope' entered my mind, and I thought, 'He's a hopeless case when it comes to being ready on Saturday afternoons, and that's the way he is.' It helped me to remember the times when I was late because I was scattered or overwhelmed. The irritation dissolved, I swept the kitchen floor, put away the laundry, and was able to smile and say a heartfelt welcome when he walked in the door. The script would have called for me to be mad and for him to feel guilty, which would have set the tone for a miserable time together."

When we abandon hope, we derail those deeply grooved ruts we create with our predictable responses. We start to accept the whole package deal of our beloved. This doesn't mean we should play the martyr, or never let our loved ones know what bothers us. It's that we speak in the spirit of revealing ourselves, not changing our partner. We recognize that people usually will continue to do

what they do, and we can either be upset about it or accept it—
possibly with a smile.

SUFFERANCE

*The marriage comes first. All other people and events come after
the marriage. Children, parents, work, and play all benefit most
by marital priority instead of marital sacrifice, because the marriage is the central unit to all other processes.*
— *Paul Pearsall*, SUPER MARITAL SEX

The definition of sufferance is: "A sanctioning to act or do
something that is granted by one in authority." In an enduring relationship, the "one in authority" is the commitment to the
union: we want this bond, this connection, this mystical, intangible experience of having something more than each of us could
have separately. The marriage is the anchor, the home base, the
center of the wheel of life. We find sustenance in it, value it, and
are fed by it. Our desire to protect this special union helps still our
criticism, own up to our insensitivity, apologize, and forgive. It
helps us stretch ourselves to give and be honest. In doing so, both
members of the union become more of who they are, and thus
bring more vitality to the relationship.

FORTITUDE, GRIT, STRENGTH

First of all, the practice [of the art of loving] requires discipline.
— *Erich Fromm*, THE ART OF LOVING

Fortitude, grit, and strength are embedded in a commitment to
be "in" life, to meet whatever happens as a couple, and to provide

a shelter for each other. Maggie spoke of the problems that arose from her undiagnosed depression.

"For years, I didn't know that when I'd get distant or cold and want to withdraw, it was depression. This was a great burden for both of us. He was most faithful, and weathered my mood swings, which could change rapidly for no apparent reason. I thought whatever was lacking was Mark's fault, and I'd blame him. My brain just had to have some reason for these crazy feelings. His response was initially anger, but we both valued each other so much that we got through it. We were awfully glad when we made up, and we always did."

For the partners I interviewed, it was truly for richer for poorer, in sickness and in health. Sometimes, the difficulties stretched over several years with troubled children, financial problems. Yet they met problems as a team. As one couple said, "We always assumed we were in it for the long haul. We never entertained the idea of leaving. When we faced hard times, we just stayed with it. It wasn't always easy, but we loved each other and had a strong bond that held us together."

PATIENCE, APPRECIATION, AND KEEPING CONNECTED

"Thanks for putting up with me all these years."
—Brian, in a forty-two-year marriage

Happily married couples foster a steady current of connection by voicing heartfelt appreciation for each other. It might be a touch, a thank-you, a favorite kind of apple from the store, a poem, or various terms of endearment. Often, it was simply acknowledging what the other person did—prepare a favorite meal, fix things around the house, get up at night to soothe a crying infant. Some of the deepest appreciation was expressed to a partner for sticking it out through tough times, or in a situation when one person was ill or bad-tempered.

Here are some words of appreciation by long-term partners:

"Linda lived through years of my traveling and building a career when we had small children. Looking back, I don't know how she managed."

"Mark called or sent a card every day when I took our daughter to the Mayo Clinic for nearly four weeks. We were always in touch."

"Margaret was totally supportive and didn't complain when I quit my awful job and went back to school. We moved into a smaller place and lived on a shoestring."

"Haley constantly tells me wonderful things about myself and shows appreciation. I'm still surprised because my second wife was so critical of me. Even talking about it right now, I'm embarrassed."

"He encouraged me to get up and give a talk in church when I was incredibly scared of speaking in front of people. He was so proud of me."

"She taught me about canoe river trips and backpacking, which I had never done."

"He listens to me gripe and complain about my mother ad nauseam. I don't know if I could put up with what I hand him." Danielle's acknowledgment of her husband's patience underscored another trait of long-term couples, namely their ability to reflect on themselves and describe their not-so-wonderful traits, put themselves in their partner's shoes, and show open appreciation.

Appreciation that comes from the heart can feel like a soothing balm. But it must be genuine—don't *try* to be pleasant when you are feeling angry or stubborn. In troubled marriages, conversations more often centered around what the partner *didn't* do. Instead of a stream of appreciation and care, there was a painful current of criticism, disapproval, withdrawal, and sharp words, leaving the spouse feeling that whatever he or she did was not enough or never quite right. It was as if a warehouse of fear, hurt, and anger stood in the way. To explore our resistance to giving means feeling whatever wounds are hidden in our heart. We need to meet our mistrust and hurt so we can find our tenderness and become generous in acknowledging our partner.

Showing appreciation is the food of love: "You matter so much to me, what a lucky person I am to be with you." We put it out there, no holding back, no protecting our heart or waiting to say kind words on cue. We offer our appreciation without asking for anything in return.

OPPOSITION-RESISTANCE

Your soul is oftentimes a battlefield, upon which your reason and your judgment wage war against your passion and your appetite. . . .

For reason, ruling alone, is a force confining; and passion, unattended, is a flame that burns to its own destruction.
—*Kahlil Gibran,* THE PROPHET

Just as we have internal parts of us pulling against each other, opposition and resistance are natural and necessary to any vital relationship. If we allow our differences to surface, cease placating our partner, or stop withdrawing, we will sometimes feel resistance or opposition in our relationships. If we can regard conflict as the other side of peace, calm, and integrity, it might help us engage with our partner as opposed to withdrawing or hiding the tension under a plastic smile.

Working through tension and resistance often leads to a more profound closeness, because we have revealed deeper levels of ourselves. When we find ways to handle differences, there's a sense of pride—hey, we're a team, we solved the problem. We didn't get burned by the fire after all, we were transformed by it.

Haley commented, "If Paul gets angry, I feel complimented. It means he trusts me, and I *want* him to be honest. I *want* to know what he's feeling. Also, if I don't like something, I say it straight out. I don't want to constantly monitor what I say. This way everything gets cleared out immediately."

The sparkle, warmth, and humor that danced so easily between Haley and Paul was testament to the love and freedom couples experience when they live together in the heart of the truth.

The ability to be open and relax into a relationship becomes easier as we step back from rules and images of what we think *should* be, and allow ourselves to respond spontaneously in the moment. From a Zen perspective, such an open mind is sometimes called a "beginner's mind."

5 DISCOVER THE FREEDOM OF BEGINNER'S MIND

The Zen way of calligraphy is to write in the most straightforward, simple way as if you were a beginner, not trying to make something skillful or beautiful, but simply writing with full attention as if you were discovering what you were writing for the first time; then your full nature will be in your writing.
—*Richard Baker, in the introduction to*
Shunryu Suzuki, ZEN MIND, BEGINNER'S MIND

Imagine rediscovering your beloved for the first time every day—not trying to make anything special, amazing, or perfect, but simply being totally present, as if you were newly experiencing each other and bringing your full nature to your relationship. To be free to meet in such an open, clear way requires a mind free of expectations, thoughts, and images.

Buddhism reminds us that "the expert" has no room to learn, while a beginner's mind is free to know everything. Having numerous rigid beliefs makes listening and learning frightening because we risk shattering these tightly held structures of the mind we think are us. We see through the thick lens of our beliefs. Conversely, if our thoughts and beliefs are porous and formless like clouds, and not identified with the self, we can look into the eyes of our beloved and, resonating with all our senses, see beneath the surface and into his or her heart and spirit.

*Instead of clinging to beliefs and opinions, if you begin to
question whether they are essential to one's comprehension of
life, then . . . one begins to dissolve one's own resistances,
which cause conflict and pain.*

— *J. Krishnamurti,* THE BOOK OF LIFE

It is so hard for a Western mind to get beyond itself, and realize that connection and spirit are embedded in experience, not in
concepts and ideas. But because love is an experience beyond
words, it is crucial to go beyond the mind to fully experience
relationships. If we have a picture of how we want our partner to look, believe, make love, or talk, we start squeezing
her or him into the straitjacket of our creation rather than forg-
ing a true connection by simply experiencing each other in the
present.

Shunryu Suzuki, a Zen Buddhist, first introduced the phrase
"beginner's mind" in *Zen Mind, Beginner's Mind,* in 1970.

*Zen mind is one of those enigmatic phrases used by Zen teach-
ers to throw you back upon yourself, to make you go behind the
words themselves and begin wondering. "I know what my own
mind is," you tell yourself, "but what is Zen mind?" And then:
"But do I really know what my own mind is? Is it what I am
doing now? Is it what I am thinking now?" And if you should
then try to sit physically still for a while to see if you can discover just what your mind is, to see if you can locate it—then
you have begun the practice of Zen, then you have begun to realize the unrestricted mind. This innocence of this first inquiry—
just asking what you are—is BEGINNER'S MIND.*

— *Introduction to* ZEN MIND, BEGINNER'S MIND

In Western culture, we are taught to gather knowledge and to use logic to "figure things out," or "*make* a relationship work." From a Zen Buddhist perspective, we need to stand back from the mind and prior learning, and resonate with experience.

How do we move toward beginner's mind? First, we realize that a belief is just a belief, a form of energy, not something concrete or solid. We also realize that our minds are conditioned with thoughts and beliefs based on memories from the past. Starting very early in life, our beginner's mind gets submerged under admonitions such as: "No, no, you shouldn't paint the sky green." "Don't put the doll's pants on her head." "What a sweet girl, so helpful." "Big boys don't cry." "This is good, this is bad," and so on.

Based on our perceptions of how we were treated, we came to conclusions about ourselves such as: I'm unlovable, unworthy, invisible, or powerless, and amassed a cobweb of interrelated thoughts and beliefs and absorbed them into our identity—I am this, I am that, I, I, I. Slowly, we became imprisoned in a little cell called "me" that was separate from others.

Rumi writes, "Beyond ideas, there is a field, will you meet me there?" Will you see me without filters or fixations or illusions? Don't make me special, just see me, understand me, be with me. Experience the passing moment here by my side. Being free of images and perceptions and expectations is the path to being in full relationship with another person.

A powerful way to access beginner's mind is the use of what Stephen Wolinsky calls the quantum question. "Without mind, memory, perceptions, interpretations, beliefs, or expectations, what is . . . happiness? . . . What is love? What's happening inside of me? What are we arguing about?" When you ask yourself this question, go slowly, imagining your mind, memory, and perceptions dissolving into thin air. You may feel yourself going blank or dropping back into an empty space, because without mind, memory, and perceptions, we have no words for our experience. It's just whatever is happening in the moment.

You might remember an experience that was so rich and amazing that you didn't want to talk about it or dull the wonder of it by reducing it to words. As we stop identifying with our thoughts, we become freer to invent, create, and take delight in the simple pleasures of life. Daily events continue to bring pleasure because we are constantly living an experience for the first time. This is reflected in Walt Whitman's poem *Leaves of Grass.*

> *I believe a leaf of grass is no less than the journeywork of the*
> *   stars . . .*
> *And the running blackberry would adorn the parlors of heaven,*
> *and the narrowest hinge in my hand puts to scorn all*
> *   machinery . . .*
> *And I could come every afternoon of my life*
> *to look at the farmer's girl boiling her iron tea-kettle and baking*
> *   shortcake.*
>
> —*Walt Whitman,* LEAVES OF GRASS

With a *beginner's mind,* we can "come every afternoon" of our life to our beloved, our friends, the flowers, the trees, to see them anew. In our relationships, a beginner's mind supersedes our immediate impulse to analyze, interpret, or judge our partner. We listen with interest and respond with a nod of the head or a few words of recognition—"Hmm, wow, that's too bad"—instead of rushing in with comments and advice all based on our past assumptions and beliefs. With an empty mind, free of worry and fear, we experience a wellspring of freedom flowing through a re-lationship, rather than getting caught in ritualized ruts and pre-dictable conversations.

Developing a beginner's mind does not mean we cease our daily tasks, or stop bringing up concerns with our lover. It means that we breathe space into our beliefs, feelings, and wants. We can learn to step back, smile at our dramas, and see our part in creating them. We might have a lively, even heated discussion, but in the backdrop of our minds, we remember we are simply ac-tors in a play, reciting our lines, engaged in a momentary dance of words and ideas that are no more than that.

As we ground ourselves in experience rather than thought, we may experience a wide array of emotions rising up. We also may feel a quiet happiness and desire for simplicity creeping into our lives. From this quiet place, we can look into our lover's eyes and, with *our* eyes, pose the question, Who are you? And be calm enough to hear the answer. This will give us a glimpse of free-dom—a spaciousness beyond words, concepts, and beliefs, a place where we can rest quietly in a stillness that is at once receptive and free. It is a simple place, not extraordinary in any way.

6 TUNE IN TO YOURSELF, TUNE IN TO YOUR LOVER

I have instant conductors all over me whether I pass
  or stop
They seize every object and lead it harmlessly
  through me
I merely stir, press, feel with my fingers, and am
  happy,
To touch my person to someone else's is about as
  much as I can stand.

—*Walt Whitman,* LEAVES OF GRASS

With a beginner's mind, we attune to ourselves and people and situations around us. We become receptive with all of our senses—we take in body language, tone of voice, speed of movement, tightness of the body, depth of breathing. It's not that we have a checklist or judge ourselves or another, it's that all our conductors are turned on. This gives us an internal sense of safety, because we can assess more clearly a situation and our reaction to it. Our body becomes the barometer of truth. We can tune in to ourselves and our lovers by saying things like: "That feels like a great idea—sounds like fun." "I don't feel drawn to doing that." "I just got tight in my stomach when you said that."

We don't need to have words to know that something doesn't feel right, we just report our uneasiness or sensations, kind of like the weather report.

It's useful to differentiate between being attuned to another person and being hypervigilant—a common trait among children brought up in troubled families where the threat of physical or emotional violence was present. Hypervigilance is a protective stance born of fear. Our fight-or-flight system is perpetually alert for cues that signal danger. This defensive survival stance, which is highly stressful, is often carried out at the expense of reflecting inwardly to the source of our fear. It becomes hardwired in the nervous system and generalized to any similar situation. As adults, we remain hypervigilant for cues that signal we are not being loved, appreciated, cared about, helped enough. It's as if we see everything through a skewed filter based on the past and notice only what fits our limited self-definition.

Attunement comes from a relaxed, receptive state motivated by a desire to know, understand, and resonate with ourselves and another person. The purpose is connection, not safety. With hypervigilance, the scanner is directed outwardly. With attunement, we are resonating with ourself *and* another person.

To experience being attuned to yourself, take a breath and release it fully, relax your shoulders, soften your belly, and drop back a bit inside so your view is more internal. Then scan your body as if you were going through it with a little flashlight, for tension, calm, fear, thoughts, judgments, and places that feel light and free. Attunement is like learning to play the instrument of you.

All musicians start their first lesson with one note, one tiny melody, but with daily practice, they learn to play a complex composition. It's the same with learning to attune to the instrument of yourself. Take a little time every day to listen to yourself as a form of meditation. One friend set his watch to go off every hour of the day so he could take a deep breath, exhale deeply, and ask, What am I feeling? It probably took twelve minutes a day, but it changed his life. Ultimately, attunement is a current of awareness running through our lives that draws us together in relationship as we shed our coverings and enter in the stream of life together.

Couples become more attuned to each other by simply asking, "How was your day?" "How did that tough talk with the boss go?" "What's been on your mind?" *By asking questions and listening carefully to our partner, we help them listen more deeply to themselves.*

There is utter magic in listening with all your senses. I have a friend who listens with complete attention, stillness, soft brown eyes, and a steady gaze. It's as if he is empty of thought and completely receiving what I say. I sometimes feel self-conscious because I hear myself so clearly. It leads me to be more mindful of what I am saying, to focus and get to the heart of my thoughts. When we hear each other from this deep stillness, it's as if we breathe into another's heart, and in doing so, we dissolve into union. We glance through the window of spirit into the heart of another. Sometimes, a smile, a concerned look, a nod, or a laugh tells our friend or lover, I am with you, I hear you.

PART TWO

I, YOU, AND US:
A DANCE IN THREE PARTS

7 EXPERIENCE THE "US" PLACE OF RELATIONSHIP: BECOMING MORE THAN WE COULD BE ALONE

The primary word I-Thou *can only be spoken with the whole being.*

—*Martin Buber,* I AND THOU

To be in true relationship requires two evolving people who attend to the trinity of *I, You,* and *Us.* This is a developmental process that started at birth. For our first six months, we thought we were merged with our mother. Everyone around was there to provide for our needs. At about six to nine months, we went through the shock of learning we were actually a separate person, and not the center of the universe—our mother cared about other people. Over time, we started to realize that we couldn't always have our way, we had to wait, share with others, and sometimes our parents or caregivers weren't smiling and happy. Hopefully, with understanding and kindness, we slowly learned that being part of the "us" could be positive and worth the sacrifice of always having our way.

The dance and challenge of balancing I, You, and Us permeated our lives as we grew up: in school, clubs, teams, and activities, we repeatedly faced various conflicts between belonging to a group and being true to ourselves. Sometimes, we belonged to a group at the expense of muffling our feelings and thoughts; other times, we stayed true to ourselves and felt alienated and alone.

Hopefully, we eventually gravitated toward people with whom we could be our authentic selves and also belong. While some found an easy fit in their early years, others didn't find a cohesive, validating group until late teens, college, or much later . . . or, perhaps, never.

For some, the idea of being true to oneself had already been submerged beneath strict indoctrination in a rigid set of beliefs and behaviors that was used as a measure of loyalty to parents. Instead of evolving our own beliefs and values based on experience and observations, we swallowed what we were taught and it became fixed inside us. We began to operate based on a litany of rules and shoulds. We drifted further and further away from ourselves.

To create the trinity of I, You, and Us, we need enough of a separate self so we are not unduly afraid of being swallowed up or absorbed by the other person. Without this, we are afraid. We tend to hold back, give halfway, and feel split in two—one foot in and one foot out of the relationship. If we feel secure enough to give ourselves fully to another without fear of being absorbed, we remain whole within the relationship. *That is the foundation of the "us" place—two well-formed people who can be separate yet able to merge into union with each other.*

With a supportive "us" place, we become more together than either of us could be alone. It's a form of alchemy, the mixing and transformation of two substances into something new: the seed and water become the plant. We become the shared body, the shared heart, which opens the window into experiencing the vastness of love and connection. Long-term couples weave their lives together, intertwining the threads of their different temperaments, needs, interests, energy levels, and passions. They often know what the other is thinking, they resonate together, yet they have separate identities. Within this warm embrace of "us," people feel safe revealing their fears, joys, and concerns because the bond is solid enough to handle whatever strong emotions arise. This in turn unites people profoundly.

With truly happy couples, it is clear that the marriage is paramount to both of them. No matter how demanding their careers or how strong their individual interests, the relationship is primary, the bedrock of their lives. People who experience a strong sense of "us" treasure it, and tend it well—like a prized garden, like a jewel.

The "us" consciousness that permeates a loving relationship will naturally extend beyond the relationship—to experiencing ourselves as part of a greater "us"—the giant web of life that is intricately interconnected.

Kahlil Gibran says it another way in *The Prophet*:

Give your hearts, but not into each other's keeping.
For only the hand of Life can contain your hearts.

When a relationship is contained by the "hand of Life," it is not an isolated unit of two people. It is two people becoming unified as they journey together, both as a couple and as part of a greater whole.

8 EXPERIENCE LIVING IN AN "US" PLACE

You drive me away gently
as a flute-song does a dove
from the eaves.

With the same song
You call me back

You push me out on many journeys;
then You anchor me with no motion at all.
                    —*Rumi*, LIKE THIS

The "us" place comes alive when we join together wanting the best for each other. It's a mentality or consciousness that allows us to simultaneously consider our needs and the best interests of our relationship or partner. It's not that we sacrifice ourselves for the relationship, but we negotiate our needs together, trusting that our partner wants us to expand and be happy.

In my interviews with long-term, happily married couples, they exuded a kind of weathered comfort that comes from knowing each other well. The "us" came for the interview, along with two separate people. The constant exchange of knowing looks, laughter, and touches revealed a wealth of connection points. Couples quibbled about details of how they met, were curious to hear the responses of the other, and frequently made humorous remarks about themselves.

Each couple was a unique composition, with its own special qualities and rhythm. With Liz and Charles, it was a quick-paced point, counterpoint, as they broke in on each other, cracking jokes, disputing what the other said, almost always with laughter or a glint in their eyes. When Charles said, "I'm not good at being social like Liz," Liz rejoined quickly, "Charles, you're very good with people." "But not like you—you make friends with everyone," was the swift reply. Another couple, Dan and Jessie, were more like two long melodies woven together. One would listen intently while the other spoke, then respond thoughtfully. They had taken part in a couples' enrichment program and had subsequently become facilitators.

With all the couples, there was an easy flow of praise and validation. In talking about their shared love for attending women's college basketball games, Liz commented with a smile, "Maybe Charles like women's basketball because he enjoys looking at beautiful women." He blushed and laughed, turning toward Liz. "It's true, I do," he said, putting his hand on her knee and looking fondly in her eyes. "That's why I married you."

Whether they were describing when they met, bringing up children, death of parents, or their sexual union, the language of these couples affirmed their bond. It was as if they were saying, Our relationship belongs to both of us. It is *our* union, *our* marriage, *our* love, *our* life together, and we both take responsibility for it.

9 CREATE MORE "US" CONSCIOUSNESS

If you feel the "us" bond is shaky in your relationship, I have listed some actions you can take to help strengthen your bond. As with any behavior, you need to understand the purpose in adopting it, so you are not simply following rote advice. If you attempt a new behavior just to do the right thing, it will feel false. On the other hand, if you have loving intent, it will shine through any awkwardness you might feel.

It is often useful to take one or two items that stand out for you and make them your focus for several months. For example, if you tend to withdraw, keep a daily log, noting the situations that tend to trigger this reaction. Ask yourself, What's going on with me? What am I afraid of? Is there really danger here, or is it just an automatic reaction? Then say to your partner, "I'm sorry I started withdrawing; it had nothing to do with you. I'm trying to be more aware so I can be more present with you."

Approach these ideas in the spirit of experimentation, to deepen your awareness and connection. At their heart, most of these suggestion are about giving up attachments, moving through fear, and being present in the moment.

1. *Think of what you have to gain by creating an "us" place.*

Imagine a deep sense of ease and closeness, of feeling connected and free inside. If thoughts of giving up your freedom come to mind when you imagine being closer, think of the warmth and joy that come from giving, loving, feeling securely united with another person.

2. *Learn the language and mind-set of "us."*

The mind-set of "us" arises as you feel the presence of your partner dwelling within your heart. Because you value and appreciate your union you automatically think about the impact of your behavior on your partner. Your desire to do what you want is tempered by thinking about how it will affect your relationship. Has she been alone at home for days with a young child? Does he need some time alone with you? With an "us" mind-set, we never take our partner for granted. We tend to our relationship on a steady basis, not because we should, but because it feeds the wellspring of our love. We delight in bringing joy to our partner.

With an "us" consciousness, we come together in the spirit of finding solutions for the couple, as opposed to accusations that imply, "You're doing it wrong." For example, saying, "I'd like to talk about *our* sex life," contains awareness of the couple as a system, as opposed to "I don't like how *you* make love to me." Other phrases from an "us" place include: "Can *we* sit down and plan our weekend?" "Can *we* talk about the way we're parenting the children?" "Can *we* come to some agreement on how *we* take care of household chores?"

3. *Repeatedly ask the question "Am I creating closeness or separation?"*

If you find yourself criticizing, judging, or mentally listing your partner's faults, think about how you would feel in your partner's place. Look in your partner's eyes when you criticize. What do you see? How does her or his body react? What is the predictable response? Then reflect on yourself. Are you hurting? Do you need something?

Take time to remember your beloved is a precious life, another tender soul just like you, imperfect and human. Think of a more gentle way to say what you need. For example, instead of snarling, "Must you spend so much time on the phone!" say, "Could you save some time for me tonight without answering the phone? I'd like to be with you." Start noticing the difference between feeling close or distant. How does it feel in your body? In your heart? Do you know when you're afraid? We need to understand relationships as an ecosystem in which everything affects everything else. Our voice, our stance, our words, our behavior either create a flow in the relationship or create stress. Nothing remains static.

4. *Avoid unilateral announcements or decisions.*

Making a unilateral decision often creates an unpleasant shock that puts your partner in a double bind. By unilateral decision, I mean taking action or making a decision without first talking it over with your partner. It could be making a major purchase, quitting a job, inviting people to stay with you, or planning to be away for an extended period of time. A unilateral decision traps your partner into the double bind of compliance or defiance. When we comply we often deny our needs and build up resentments; if we defy we risk appearing as the "heavy," or being disagreeable, or starting an argument.

Avoiding unilateral decisions applies to the small daily things as well as major decisions about jobs, houses, and babies. Here's an example: A unilateral decision could be that you walk into the living room where your partner is reading and turn on the TV. Your partner is put in the position of either putting up with it, or saying, "I really don't want the TV on." This could be the start of a fight. On the other hand, if you say, "I'd like to watch a TV program. Is that okay with you?," you remain in the "us" place. Then you can seek a solution. Maybe you can put the TV in the bedroom, or get earphones, or compromise on how long it's on. The point is that you've take action in the spirit of "us."

5. *Listen beneath the surface of a behavior . . . and look for the positive intention.*

Ken Keyes, author of *Handbook to Higher Consciousness*, teaches that there is a positive intention underlying our behavior—usually the desire to feel loved, connected, powerful, affirmed, comforted, or to ease our pain. When we become insistent and repeat ourselves, our positive intention is to be heard. We withdraw with the positive intention of hiding our embarrassment, we talk compulsively to cover up our insecurity, yell to cover up our shame, or give unsolicited advice because we want to connect or feel useful and important. All these behaviors may be unskillful or irritating, but they rarely have malicious intent. If we can listen beneath the surface for the positive intention, we may feel less reactive and more understanding—which helps us feel compassionate rather than separate.

We can apply the concept of the positive intention both to ourselves and others. If we lose our temper, are dishonest, give unsolicited advice, get bossy or scared, we can ask ourselves, What was my positive intention under this? What do I need? Was it appropriate? How can I be more direct? We can reflect on our actions rather than getting caught in a circle of judgment and self-criticism that usually leads to repeating the same unwanted behavior.

If we listen for the positive intention in others, we can help ease a difficult situation by asking, "What would you like from me?" "How can I be helpful?" "Is this what you were trying to say?" When we learn to reach out to the confusion and pain of each other, we meet each other in the "us" place and move toward the heart of understanding, rather than reacting at a superficial level.

6. *Take comfort in your bond. Pull together instead of isolating.*

Many people tend to withdraw when they are upset. An old reflex goes off—I'm too embarrassed, afraid, or ashamed to be seen. As an experiment to increase your bond, the next time you feel hurt or upset, resist the desire to isolate yourself and instead ask your partner to stay near you.

You might experiment with sitting together in silence asking for guidance, or having your partner touch you. Caring touch sends an immediate message to the brain and nervous system that can help transform conditioned beliefs. For example, "I feel hurt, therefore I'm bad" can become "I'm hurt, and I can be comforted." If we continuously isolate ourselves when we're hurt, we harden our belief that being hurt makes us unworthy. Moreover, in staying connected, not only do you gain comfort, you allow your partner to join you and in so doing bring deeper meaning to the "us" place.

This is not to imply that there aren't times when you want to be apart or to take a few minutes alone to gather yourself or calm down, but the more you can find ways to connect through your pain and differences, the more you will feel the soft spot in your heart and realize that you are not alone.

7. *Open up and talk about yourself.*

To intertwine ourselves together as a couple, we need to talk about our daily experiences. It doesn't matter if we're clumsy, awkward, or unskillful in speaking; just open up and talk about yourself. It's a way of saying, I'm here with you, you matter to me. Talk about your day—what were you thinking about? What was fun? What was disappointing? What's new with the people you work with? How did that talk with the boss go? Reveal your fears, insecurities, and doubts as well as your successes. If this is difficult because you go blank, you can always start by saying, "I feel blank." "I'm scared." "I feel like such a boring person." Anything. Don't be silent and unresponsive. You can even say, "It's not that I don't care, but I'm never sure what to say." Almost anyone will be sympathetic toward such a revelation.

The other side of the equation is to listen to your partner in the spirit of knowing and connecting. There's no need to comment, give advice, or question your partner's behavior. Just listen.

If the "us" place feels like a foreign concept, it's likely there is unfinished hurt or trauma from the past that has led you to be self-protective or self-absorbed. Psychotherapy or counseling may be helpful for exploring old patterns and softening the protective armor that makes it frightening to enter the "us" place or relinquish your separate self. Some people have fought so hard to survive, it feels terrifying to let go and become vulnerable to another. It feels almost impossible to believe that you can be vulnerable and yet still safe.

You can remind yourself, *That was then, this is now.* Notice your feelings, your body; breathe. Stay in the present.

Test the "us" place in little ways. Reveal something slightly personal about yourself and see what happens. Then take another little step. And another. You won't always get the response you'd like, but you will be more alive because you've opened the door to your inner world and you will feel more complete as a result.

10 FEEL THE HEALING POWER OF CONNECTION

I belong to the beloved,
have seen the two worlds as one . . .
first, last, outer, inner, only that
breath breathing human being.
— *Rumi,* THE ESSENTIAL RUMI

The rewards of coming into full relationship with your partner are many. As you read the following synonyms of "enduring," take in their meaning: *abiding, continuing, unceasing, perennial, indelible, indissoluble, invincible.*

Ideally, a loving union can provide both an anchor *and* freedom. While nothing in life is secure, a bonded relationship provides a dependable home base—a place with loving arms to greet you, and someone to cheer for you as you expand and grow. In a trusting relationship, you don't wake up with a knot in your gut, or worry if she or he will show up after work, or carry through on agreements. You know you get to make mistakes, be imperfect, and still be loved. This home base of trust and care helps people feel more confident to venture into new territory, both within themselves and in the world.

Not all long-term relationships attain this desirable enduring state. Some relationships look more like a feat of endurance than a vital, alive bond that brings pleasure. Others resemble a polite, cooperative agreement to live as friends but not lovers. The couple may care deeply about each other and be cooperative, but they lack the depth that comes from revealing themselves fully to each other.

A Buddha marriage is not a feat of survival—it's a means for opening, reflecting, deepening love, compassion, and awareness, and experiencing the healing power of connection. The connection that comes with an enduring relationship is the most powerful healer on the planet, and through it lies a powerful antidote to alienation, stress, and anxiety. It is also good for our health.

> One health risk factor that underlies all the others is a sense of
> isolation, loneliness, a feeling of being disconnected.
> —Paul Pearsall, SEXUAL HEALING

Buddhists talk about the butterfly effect—namely, the fluttering of a butterfly's wings, with its subtle vibration emanating out to the whole world, affecting everything. Every word, every kindness, every touch, every action, carries a vibration of energy that is transmitted to the people around us. Depression, anxiety, frenetic activity, fear, anger all penetrate the atmosphere of our dwelling place. If we think of our immune system and body as an ecosystem whose health is attuned to our physical and emotional environment, we can understand to some degree the amazing power of a loving, honest connection.

If all this sounds esoteric or hard to grasp, simply think of a time you experienced a peaceful, effortless flow between you and another person. It might have been a conversation you wove together—listening, responding, laughing, becoming spontaneous, as you relaxed deeper and deeper inside yourself, feeling more attuned to your friend or lover. When we enter such a state, it often feels as if time slows down, or, paradoxically, that the hours slip by. If you can recall such a memory and bring it to mind, including the sounds, smells, colors, air, your body will slow down as your cells, muscles, and nervous system relax. Perhaps a warmth or soft feeling will gently radiate in your chest. Meanwhile, your immune system will respond to this soothing memory by renewing itself.

PART THREE

LOOK IN YOUR OWN MIRROR

11 RECOGNIZE THE MASKS YOU WEAR

"I can't explain myself, I'm afraid, sir, because I'm not myself, you see."
— *Lewis Carroll,* ALICE IN WONDERLAND

Wherever you are on the path of self-exploration, it helps to remember that we are all wearing costumes. As children, many of us put on masks to fit a certain image—good boy, good girl, nice, quiet, charming, tough, smart, generous, and so on. Unfortunately, if that mask becomes crucial to our survival, it can get glued on so tightly that it starts to feel real. As a result, we end up navigating through life separated from our authentic self. The more we become conscious of the masks we have donned, however, and the more willing we are to take them off, the more we create trust, safety, and honesty in a relationship.

The first step in taking off your mask is realizing it's there. An exercise I have found useful is to dramatize your masks. In workshops I suggest that people mill around a room and go through a list of common personas—being charming, angry, seductive, flirtatious, coy, crazy, and so on. With each persona, I ask them to walk around for a while, then freeze and notice the sensations in their bodies—is it strong, tight, flat? People will say, that one was easy, or that another one was embarrassing or very foreign. This helps people realize that if we can step into a role, we can also step out of it.

I do a similar exercise with couples. For example, one partner can be the needy one begging for love and attention, and the other can react to it. One can experiment with being withdrawn or depressed, while the other partner tries to cheer him or her up. Then they switch roles. The result of these exercises is a tremendous opening of energy, and awareness that we are, in fact, playing roles much of the time.

For over twenty years, Tom and Jody played out several roles in their relationship. Jody was the mothering, responsible, limit-setting one, as in "No, we can't afford that." Tom, meanwhile, was the compliant-defiant boy who liked mothering, spent money impulsively, and was playful, warm, and creative. They both were capable of a wide range of feelings but were extremely eager to relieve the gnawing emptiness they each felt underneath their masks.

We started by exploring Jody's "mothering" mask, which complemented Tom's boy-who-likes-mothering mask. They chose to act out a scene in which Tom comes home from work and bemoans in a weak, pathetic voice: "I had such a hard day, people were demanding so much, I'm *so* tired. I—"

Jody broke in, her voice shifting into a smooth, velvet tone, "Oh, honey, you just sit down. Can I bring you some soup or tea or something?"

As they continued, their smiles widened until they both burst out laughing.

Then Jody said, in her normal voice, "I feel ridiculous. This is so silly. I can't believe we've been doing this for so long."

Tom smiled at her.

"You guys are really good," I said. "Tom, how old did you feel?"

"Oh, about eight." He laughed again. "I love thinking about what age I am. It makes things so clear."

I then asked, "How could you get your needs met without the

old masks?" I suggested Jody wait until Tom asked for what he really wanted. It took a couple of tries, but eventually it came up like this:

Tom came in and, in a "grown-up" voice, said, "I'm tired. What a day."

Jody looked at him with a smile. "Really. Tough day."

Tom: "Yeah." Pause. "Could you get me something to drink?"

"I could do that," Jody replied. "What do you want?"

Big pause, followed by, "What I really want is a hug."

"Sure."

By agreeing to reveal their masks and role-play with each other, Tom and Jody interrupted the collusive game they had both tacitly agreed to play. What they discovered was that their roles had become so ingrained that they become automatic: "I act pathetic and you take care of me." "I mother you, so you won't leave," and so on.

By taking off their masks, they opened the way to a deeper exploration of inner, authentic selves. Jody mothered Tom because she had a deep, underlying belief that she was worthless and had to buy love by giving lavish attention. Tom loved being mothered at one level, but resented it at another. But as they removed their masks together, laughing and embracing, they took a giant step into the "us" place.

If you and your partner are stuck in a predictable argument, try acting it out by switching roles. Then play your original role and exaggerate it. Get truly dramatic, and feel it in your whole being. It may seem embarrassing, but if you can do it in the spirit of becoming visible to yourself, and your partner, it can be extremely revealing—even amusing. There's something wondrously freeing about owning up to the games we play, and stepping out from behind a mask. And the very fact of doing it together will help bring you closer. One might say that freedom is what happens when there's nothing left to hide.

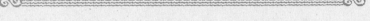

12 ASK YOURSELF, "AM I TALKING ABOUT MYSELF?"

The full moon is inside your house.
—*Rumi,* "Be Melting Snow"

Most people want to be less judgmental. The first step to awareness comes from recognizing that our judgments of others often reflect judgments of ourselves. The next time you find yourself being critical by thinking someone is insensitive, dishonest, unkind, stop for a moment and ask, "Am I talking about myself?" If I repeatedly judge others as being uncaring, is it because I sometimes have difficulty caring about others? If I feel critical of my partner for acting helpless with her demanding boss, I can reflect and ask, "Are there ways I act helpless?"

Our reaction may be a clear mirror image, a similar situation with the same dynamic, or something from the past we haven't forgiven in ourselves. Either way, it's important to remember that judgments directed outward often reflect judgments of self.

You can also check the mirror by asking, "Am I feeling what I think the other person is feeling?" For example, whenever you think someone is angry at you, ask yourself, "Am I angry, or do I often hide my anger?" If you start having thoughts that your partner is having an affair (and there really is no evidence to suggest this), ask yourself, "Am I frustrated sexually and fantasizing an affair?" Don't brush away this question without a careful search. So often we want to maintain a certain image of ourselves, instead of going deep enough to connect with our true feelings, especially the ones we consider bad or wrong.

The mirror also can reveal the loving, caring parts of ourselves. Can you remember a time when you were feeling grumpy or irritated and someone was particularly understanding toward you? Your heavy mood lifted because he or she was patient and kind, which awakened a more loving, accepting part of yourself.

Successful couples are skillful at reflecting the best parts of each other, creating an upward spiral of warmth, safety, and happiness that embraces the relationship. For people who hold tenaciously to a negative image of themselves, however, it can feel uncomfortable to have their goodness and talent reflected, because it would shatter their negative self-image. We need to remember it's as egoistic to hang on to a negative self-image as to an inflated image, because they both intensify our belief of being a fixed and separate self. When we experience our beliefs as solid and dense, they obstruct our connection to our essential beingness. They also keep us from connecting personally with others.

On the spiritual journey, everyone becomes our teacher, because each provides a mirror. To become intimate implies a daily willingness to look in the mirror and see what it reveals about ourselves. If we're not willing to look, we'll want to break the mirror or push away the person whom it reflects. If we do allow ourselves to glance in the mirror, we will realize that all the things we want to hide are nothing but natural human attributes or emotions.

13 REMEMBER TO ASK, "WHO OWNS THE PROBLEM?"

In the exquisite dance of relationships, it's important to sort out whether a problem belongs to an individual or to the "us" place. Just because we are in a relationship to love and cherish each other, it doesn't mean we have to absorb each other's problems. Often, when doing therapy with a couple, I draw a line down the middle of the page and say, "Okay, now what belongs to you, what belongs to your partner, and what belongs in the 'us' place?"

For example, if one is having a quarrel with a friend, the problem belongs to him. But if he complains endlessly about it to his partner, he is affecting the "us" place he needs to take care of his troubled friendship or stop talking about it all the time. His partner can also play a role by setting limits, offering suggestions, being supportive, or all three. A response can be clear, yet made with lovingkindness: "You know, I understand you're upset with your friend, but I don't want to talk about it every night. I'm glad to support you doing something to help the situation. But I'd like a night where we talk about other things." It's like saying, I hear your problem, I care, but that's enough, please do something about it.

Oftentimes, underlying the question of who owns the problem is a developmental stage that needs to be completed. Namely, in the first few years of life, we assume we are the center of attention and that everyone is automatically fascinated by our dramas and thoughts. It usually includes a belief that if someone doesn't give us their undivided attention or doesn't want to hear about our dramas, he or she doesn't love or care about us.

We need to come into the present and remember we are adults, which implies a responsibility to address our life situation. Eckhart Tolle in *The Power of Now* reminds us that when we have a problem we have three choices—leave the situation, change the situation, or accept it completely. Otherwise it occupies tremendous energy, and keeps us from being present.

It's hard on a relationship when our frustrations continuously spill onto our partner and we make no effort to solve our concerns. Conversely, the more we clear out difficulties, the more we bring a bright spirit to our relationship and to the "us" place.

14 LIVE IN THE CENTER OF YOUR OWN LIFE

My limbs are made glorious
By the touch of this world of life.
—Rabindranath Tagore

When you immerse yourself in the stream of life and feel the rhythmic measure of your passions dancing through you, you bring vitality to your relationship and all the people around you. In turn, this contribution to the "us" place of life keeps the fires burning within you as an individual.

For some, being immersed in the stream of life may necessitate turning off the TV or computer, getting off the couch, and expanding their world by taking up some new endeavors. For others, it might mean slowing down the pace so their awareness isn't submerged in a constant buzz of activities. We may need to reevaluate how we're spending our time and focus on what enhances our life and leads us forward, while letting go of the things that pull us back or leave us depleted. The choices can be difficult, yet we need to set priorities.

Ask yourself, what brings you pleasure and helps you expand? What have you always wanted to do? When you're taking on new endeavors, remember that the purpose is not to excel or be great—although it's fun if that happens—it's to feel the pulse of your own life. This may appear self-indulgent, and not in alignment with Buddhist teachings about service to others as central to the spiritual journey. But we can't give from an empty vessel, or drink from an empty well. When we walk this earth with a light heart and a joyful spirit, we bring a special radiance wherever we go. The idea is not to "do good" or "be good," but rather to live in the heart of goodness, and follow our calling. People who experience joy and fulfillment naturally want to be of service to others.

Living in the center of our own life means we sense the river of awareness as it arises from within, act on our best guidance, and stop worrying whether it's the right decision or what other people will think. The more we flow with ourselves, the deeper we can immerse ourselves in a loving relationship. It's all the same river, the river of being alive.

15 NOTICE THE STORIES YOU TELL YOURSELF

The single most vital step on your journey toward enlightenment is this: learn to disidentify from your mind. Every time you create a gap in the stream of mind, the light of your consciousness grows stronger.

—*Eckhart Tolle,* THE POWER OF NOW

Thoughts can be loose and airy, or they can be tight, hard, and dense. The more they solidify and become concrete, the more we are separated from our experience and from those around us. Thoughts get crystallized as we repeat the stories we habitually use to explain our lives: "I can't read well because I had a mean second-grade teacher." "I can't cook because my mother was so critical when I was a child." "I eat too much because I'm afraid of intimacy." The more we repeat a story, the more it becomes rock solid in our mind, and lives in us as "the truth." The problem is this: We're not a story, we are a living, breathing, changing experience. We need to stop telling ourselves the same old tales and start resonating with the present.

In relationships, we tend to make up a story about our partner that turns into an image of who he or she is. We might idealize him, or have a negative view, or have a mixed opinion. Whatever we do, it's important to realize that we are constructing an image rather than relating in the present to this living, breathing, ever-changing person.

We first need to recognize that we are telling a story. Then we can ask ourselves, What would happen if I stopped telling the same tired old story, and engaged in the moment? This requires a willingness to bring full awareness to our feelings, thoughts, and fears. So instead of saying, "I can't cook because my mother was so crabby," invite a friend over and cook together, or pull out a recipe and do it on your own and allow yourself to experience whatever arises in the present. If you feel discomfort because of the old belief, gently tell yourself you are no longer a child. That was a long time ago.

Couples often create a story of their relationship that gets hardened: I can't tell him I'm upset because he works so hard. I can't let her know I've lost money gambling, she'll get mad. Our stories are based on perceptions and beliefs stemming from the past. They keep us from engaging consciously with our partner in the present. Couples often hang on to the story: my partner had an affair. If it's over and no longer happening, then we're just creating more pain and suffering by keeping it alive in our mind. We are losing the precious moment of now. Take a few minutes to reflect on all the stories you tell yourself about your partner that keep you apart. Then imagine letting them all go and looking in your partner's eyes and seeing who's there today.

PART FOUR

THE DAILY PRACTICE OF LIVING AND LOVING

16 TREASURE TRUST: KEEP AGREEMENTS WITH GREAT CARE

As in everything else, I must start with myself. That is: in all circumstances try to be decent, just, tolerant, and understanding, and at the same time try to resist corruption and deception. In other words, I must do my utmost to act in harmony with my conscience and my better self.

—*Vaclav Havel,* SUMMER MEDITATIONS

Successful couples keep agreements. It's natural—not because of a sense of duty, but because it's woven into the fabric of personal integrity and caring for others. Keeping agreements nurtures trust and creates a safe haven for relationships.

Being able to keep agreements also reflects self-knowledge. If someone asks me to go to a movie next Friday or on a camping trip next month, I know myself well enough to say yes, with the inner assurance that when the time comes, I'll do it and I'll enjoy it. Keeping agreements starts by making agreements mindfully. We learn to scan our interior world, do an emotional reading, and check to see if we're being realistic when we say yes. *We remember that keeping an agreement implies a commitment to do what it takes to follow through.*

Charles and Liz, married forty-four years, recalled the *one* time, shortly after they met, when Liz didn't show up for a date. She had forgotten she was scheduled to play in a baseball game that night and, not having his phone number, didn't know how to reach him to reschedule. When they met later that evening, after he had waited for over an hour, she explained and apologized. Forty-four years later, they still remember that night, because it was such a significant departure from their steadfast way of keeping agreements.

Troubled couples often have a landscape strewn with broken agreements. It's a way they keep distance. It often reflects the lack of a solid investment in the relationship and creates a chronic climate of anxiety in the partner, who is repeatedly anticipating a letdown. Neither person is free to relax into the relationship and trust their partner.

People sometimes break agreements because they feel stuck in roles. A common scenario was explained by Jeffrey: "I feel so responsible to take care of everything, and I'm trying so hard to be a good guy, that I automatically say yes to any request. Then I realize I don't want to do it, or I don't know how to do it, and I feel too embarrassed to admit how inadequate I feel—you know, I'm a man, I'm supposed to know how to do all these things—so I just 'forget' to do it and hope the problem goes away." He laughed. "Of course it doesn't."

Another common scenario happens when one partner perceives keeping agreements as being controlled or pushed around. Jenny, a client of mine, said, "Why should I always have to tell him where I'm going or what I'm doing after work? I want to be free." She eventually realized she was relating to him as a rebellious teenager does to a parent. She had not yet given birth to an "us" consciousness. Some time later, when Jenny made a commitment to be on time or call, she experienced a major shift in two ways. "It feels good to me," she said, "like something solid inside, like being a grown-up. It's also helping our relationship because Matt is nicer and we're not fighting so much."

If a relationship is deeply rooted, and both partners feel loved, an occasional change of plans won't be a problem—these things happen. But chronically changing plans or breaking agreements erodes the foundation of a relationship.

A small digression about being on time. Just as people differ in their tolerance for messiness, people have their own rhythm with regard to being on time. Some people are usually early, some are always on time, others are regularly ten minutes late, etc. For example, with a hiking group I joined, the leader explained: "We're scheduled to meet in the parking lot at eight A.M. Ed will already be there, I'll be ten minutes late, Jenny is usually about fifteen minutes late, and we leave about twenty minutes late."

We don't need to attribute interpretations to these rhythmic differences. It doesn't necessarily mean someone is ambivalent, disrespectful, unkind, and so on—it's just their rhythm. What's important in a relationship is to be clear and work out a plan to handle differences.

If you're not sure about agreeing to something, you can be straightforward: "I'm not quite sure. I'll need to think it over." "Can I say a tentative yes, and get back to you?" "I'm really feeling too stressed today, could it be done tomorrow?" If you want to keep agreements but just can't seem to manage, you might want to tune in to see if there is a rebellious teenager lurking under the surface, along with buried grief or a fear of vulnerability.

When both members of a couple are willing to explore broken agreements and make changes, tremendous healing can occur. After Jenny told Matt that she stayed away to avoid his sharp criticism, he committed to break this destructive habit. Matt undertook the psychological work of taking the halo off his parents' heads and realizing how intensely critical and absent they had been when he was a child. Once he connected with the emotional pain he had suffered, he was able to be more aware of the impact of his own behavior. As his criticism abated, albeit with slips and occasional arguments, Jenny started coming home more. The positive impact on their relationship was readily felt by both of them.

17 TUNE IN TO YOUR DEEPER MOTIVATION

Exploring our motivation is the groundwater of the spiritual path. And it's often immensely uncomfortable. It's embarrassing to reveal that we've been seductive or plied our partner with wine because we felt guilty for spending so much money. It's painful to realize that our pleading and nagging mask a desperate, childlike cry for love. It's hard to admit that we flirted with our partner's best friend because we were angry. One woman commented about her anger at her unfaithful husband: "I watched with relish as he gained twenty pounds because he couldn't resist my great cooking. Maybe then she wouldn't want him."

We often need to peel through layers of excuses and stories to find the underlying motivation for our behavior. Penny talked about a relationship in which her partner repeatedly was unnerved because she chewed with her mouth open or made a lot of noise, usually when just the two of them were having dinner together.

"He was appalled because he prided himself on being very refined. He was a wine connoisseur and excellent gourmet cook. I thought it was funny, for a while, but then, because it made him so angry, I made a commitment to him and to myself to stop. Then I couldn't stop. And I felt really upset with myself. I didn't have access to what it was about, and became very embarrassed because my conscious intention was to knock it off. It wasn't until many months later that I realized I was angry at him for giving me messages in a variety of ways that I lacked refinement and was unsuitable for elegant dinner parties because of my crass behavior. The odd thing was that I'd never done it before and have never done it since. As soon as I realized I was angry, I was able to stop. I had a choice. I could be angry with him directly, rather than provoking his anger at me."

When our motivation isn't clear, our exchanges start sounding like a scene from *Who's Afraid of Virginia Woolf?* Instead of talking about the real issues, we blame when we're afraid, cry when we're angry, ask a question when we want to make a statement. We also hide our anger with a well-placed dig, or resort to sugarcoated comments that hit with a sting rather than reveal our anger or hurt. In interviewing women in codependency groups, they often talked about how difficult it was to admit to being angry. One woman commented, "We don't want to tarnish our image of being the long-suffering wife." But images can't have relationships.

It takes humility to pry deep beneath the surface and recognize our motivation. It can help to think of our behavior as unconscious or unskillful. To become more attuned to ourselves, we go beneath our first impulses to react, and ask instead:

> What's going on with me?
> What am I really feeling?
> Am I afraid? Am I angry? Am I hurting?
> Am I really asking for what I want?
> Did I agree to do something I don't really want to do?
> Are there feelings of inadequacy underlying my words?
> How could I be more honest?
> What would be a more skillful way to handle the situation?

Once we become aware of our motivation, we need to ante up or apologize. One client would often start a session by saying, "Okay, it's true confession time," as an introduction to owning up to her behavior. For some, the thought of admitting to their mistakes fills them with the fear that the other person will respond, "You are disgusting. I'll never talk to you again." Yet, having counseled couples for twenty-five years, I can attest that the opposite usually happens.

Revealing our wounded self usually elicits understanding, because most of us know it's tough to admit to our less-than-stellar qualities. When we say, "I'm sorry. I was off base, I was really feeling angry. I apologize," it's also a great relief to the partner, who is happy to have her reality validated. It's so confusing to hear someone say, "No, I'm not angry," when our gut tells us otherwise. Owning up to "our stuff" helps us tap into the milk and honey of relationship—the golden cord that reconnects us with our beloved and takes us back into the "us" place.

18 "THAT'S NOT WHAT I SAID": NOTICE YOUR INTERPRETATIONS

Buddhism talks about clear seeing in the present. Hearing what people truly say, without adding our own interpretations, allows us to see our partner in current time rather than through the haze of our conditioned mind.

We all adopt filters through which we see the world. Some people call these our core beliefs, or false core beliefs: "I'm stupid, I'll always be left, I must be perfect, I'm second best," and so on. From this base, we spin a web of other interpretations: "If I act stupid, you won't respect me." "If you confront me, it means you don't love me."

On the path of awakening, we need to realize it is our own filters that create our interpretations of what is taking place around us. It is amazing how we can twist and rearrange what someone has said or done to prove our basic core beliefs about ourselves. We need to step back and return to reality by asking, what actually happened? What did my partner really say—verbatim? If you pay attention to the meaning you attribute to others' words, you are likely to discover the filter through which you see the world.

Elaine came for therapy complaining about her husband—he's inconsiderate, he doesn't care, he just goes off and plays poker on Friday night. I listened to her frustration for a while, then asked, "How do you know that his playing poker means he doesn't care about you?"

She paused, then said, "Because he leaves me alone and doesn't seem to care."

"But have you actually asked him, 'Are you playing poker with your friends because you don't love me?' You need to be very specific."

"Well, I haven't done that exactly, but I just know," she said, quieting down.

But we don't "just know." Our interpretations may feel very real and true, but we need to leave room for doubt. We may be putting the situation through our own personal filter. It works like this.

If Elaine could recognize that it is her filter that is determining her reaction, she opens the possibility of having a completely different response.

To help her with this, I suggested a technique that helps people pierce the fog of their interpretations. "Try saying this to yourself:

Message	Filter	Conclusion Based on Filter Response	Emotions
Jim plays poker on Friday night.	*I'm unlovable.*	*He doesn't love me.*	*Hurt*
	I'm not worthy.	*He doesn't care about me.*	*Anger*

'Ted is being Ted. Ted is doing what Ted does. Ted is cold sometimes. Ted is warm sometimes. Ted likes to play poker. That's what Ted does *and it means nothing about me.*' " She was fascinated with the assignment and agreed to do it.

The next week, Elaine arrived eager to talk. "I was doing that internal chant, 'Ted is being Ted,' and I suddenly heard, 'Elaine is being Elaine,' and I just started to cry because I felt so tender toward myself. I realize how much I've been criticizing him." She also said that she had seen Ted in a new way. "I had this flash of seeing him, just as this person, this man I live with. This guy who's struggling to do well in his work. I had the thought, 'Why am I making such a fuss about his poker playing?' " She paused and smiled. "I think I'm jealous because he enjoys it so much— they've played together for seventeen years."

Within a couple of weeks she could see herself switch in and out of the different lenses through which she saw the situation. "Sometimes I feel hurt, sometimes I'm angry, sometimes I just see this guy who wants to be with his buddies and drink beer and play poker." During our sessions, she practiced stepping in and out of these various perspectives or ego states to realize that she could turn them on and off. I'd say, "Bring up the angry part. Now bring up the 'He's just a guy who likes to play poker' part. " This crucial step of recognizing our ability to switch our perspective and experience our different filters starts the process of understanding that there are many possible reactions to a situation based on our internal filters.

One common misinterpretation is "You're controlling me." I often ask clients what they mean by this generalization. With one couple, it went like this: Margaret asked Danny if he'd like to go with her to a particular movie on Friday night. Because Danny interpreted this to mean, *I must take her or she won't love me*, he felt controlled when, in reality, she was just asking him. He was restless during the movie and in a prickly mood as they left. Margaret asked him why he was being so critical, and he spewed back, "Well, I really wanted to go out to dinner, but you're so controlling." Wisely, Margaret replied in a kind tone, "I would have been glad to go to dinner, but you didn't say anything, so I didn't know." If Danny can hear Margaret and realize that he misinterpreted her request, and it was his responsibility to voice his desires, the conflict will dissolve. "You're right, I didn't say anything, then I got mad. I'm sorry." If he defends his turf instead—"Well, you should have known!"—there will be no resolution and the wheel of suffering will roll on.

To move beyond our automatic interpretations, we need to first acknowledge that they exist. Once we can say to ourselves, "Oh, there's that 'I'm worthless' filter, or 'I'm afraid of being left' filter, or 'I'm not good enough' filter," we start to see how we are misperceiving others. The more we recognize that our filters are not who we really are, the more we can step back and see beyond them. They come from interpretations we made based on earlier experience. We took them on, but now we can recognize them and see beyond them.

19 LEARN TO TRUST YOUR INTUITION

One summer, at age ten, while standing around a primitive swimming pond at an Episcopal church camp, I watched with curiosity as my favorite counselor handed her watch and bracelet to a friend, took a few steps back, ran wildly from the edge of the woods onto the diving board and, with a great howl, leaped into the pond with her clothes on. I felt a thrill surge through me as she plunged into the water, creating a mighty splash, then surfaced with a huge smile on her face as she jostled her head to shake off the water. Like a fireworks display, her uproarious behavior brought laughter and smiles to everyone standing around the pond, including the ministers whom I saw as being elevated above me.

A few minutes later, someone dulled our collective pleasure by asking her *why* she did it. She brushed him off, laughing: "I just felt like it."

Ponder for a moment simply learning to say, *I want to, I don't want to,* or *I'm not sure,* without adding lengthy explanations. Imagine operating from a deep level of awareness, free from your internal censors. When we resonate with that inner pull, we tap into our playfulness, creativity, and wisdom. We go beyond the mind and become more truly present in life and in relationships. It's also more fun. One note of caution: Sometimes we confuse this inner pull with a trickster and con who tries to convince us to take part in some crazy scheme or indulge in drugs or food. But we can readily discern the difference if we think of the harmful consequences that will follow.

What we need to remember is that life is happening in the present moment. *Most problems or concerns will not be solved solely by thinking, creating lists, or making up stories. We may do these things as a prelude to dropping into silence and allowing the answers to surface.*

In some Buddhist meditation practices, people are taught to sit quietly and focus on their breath as it rises and falls. When the mind slips off to *What's for lunch?* or *Am I doing it right?*, the instruction is simply to say "thinking" and return to following the breath.

The more we give up reasons and stories in favor of that deep, strong pull at the center of our gut, the simpler and happier life becomes. We also become able to speak clearly and honestly about our experience in the moment.

Here are two sample conversations. In the first example, both people get trapped in making up reasons to defend what they want to do.

Example 1.
Dialogue of a couple making up stories/reasons/rationalizations:

MARIE: John, I'd really like you to go to dinner with me at the Simpsons'. They invited us for Friday.

JOHN: Oh, I don't know them very well.

MARIE: They really want to see us. They so often ask about you.

JOHN: That's hard to believe. I don't have much in common with either one of them.

MARIE: But it's good to get out and spend time with new people.

JOHN: Well, you can go. I'll be fine staying home.

MARIE (*hurt tone*): You are never interested in being with me or with the people I like.

JOHN: You're always trying to tell me what to do.

And on and on.

Example 2.

Conversation based on I want to *and* I don't want to *where each person completely accepts the response of the other. It might go something like this:*

MARIE: I want to do something special with you Friday night. The Simpsons asked us for dinner. What do you think of going there?

JOHN: I'd like to be with you Friday night, but I really don't want to spend an evening with them.

MARIE: What would you like to do together?

JOHN: Let's see. Maybe go out to dinner, or to a movie.

MARIE: Would you be willing to go to dinner and then go dancing at the Holiday Inn. There's a good group playing there.

JOHN (*first pauses*): Yes. That sounds good.

Notice in the second conversation no one questioned the other's motives or made-up stories. They simply stuck with I *want to* and I *don't want to* as it arose in the moment.

If we can trust that deep well of intuition that results in simple requests and responses, without rationalizations and reasons, we stay true to ourselves and our relationships.

20 OF LOVE AND LITTER: DEALING WITH COMPULSIONS IN RELATIONSHIPS

To be in a relationship, we often need to navigate around each other's foibles and weird little behaviors. We all use various escapes to manage tension and anxiety. In anticipation of a difficult conversation, we eat chocolate, clean the house, fix the car, talk intensely with a friend, or sleep. With many couples there is some discrepancy in the desire for order, or the tolerance for litter and messiness. While this can be irritating and sometimes difficult, it is usually negotiable if both partner have goodwill.

Compulsions, in contrast, involve chronic, often ritualistic behaviors that we use to calm ourselves and reduce tension. *We do not derive pleasure so much from the actual behavior as from the relief it provides.* As you will see from the words I have italicized, compulsions are typified by words such as *I can't, I have to,* and *I must,* and so on. While they act as a security blanket to cover troublesome feelings, they also take us deeply into a trance state so we are not present to our partner. At one end of the spectrum, there may be little rituals that surround our daily routines—we *must* have our coffee a certain way, we *can't* feel relaxed unless we read the paper or do our morning exercises. At a middle state, we *can't* relax after dinner until the kitchen is immaculate, or we are just the opposite: we are compulsively messy and just can't seem to keep things tidy, even though we would like to. Other compulsions: we *must* have a constant background of music or TV; we *must* keep busy; we *can't* relax without sex. At the far extreme, we are *driven* to work constantly, keep an immaculate house, and stay busy. *We worry incessantly and our mind is continually focused on all the troubles in the world.*

With a compulsion, there can be an intense need to have things a certain way, and woe to the person who disrupts our ritual, or uses something of ours without returning it. Using Buddhist language, you could say compulsions are highly charged attachments.

What separates a compulsion from a mere preference is the agitation and distress one feels if the compulsion is not satisfied. It's one thing to *like* an uncluttered, well-organized house; it's another to feel highly agitated and unable to relax if your house is not perfectly organized. It's one thing to *want* to get projects done; it's another to work in the garage all weekend and feel you can't stop and spend time with your family until you are completely finished. It's fine to enjoy getting accolades and good grades; it's another to feel terrible about yourself when you don't measure up to your high standards.

Because compulsions keep us preoccupied, they also create separation in relationships in several ways. First, when someone is compulsive, people around them tend to live in fear of setting them off. I remember as a child, my dad would get intensely upset if anything of his was missing—a tool, a pencil, or his comb. One time, I borrowed his small black comb from the bathroom and forgot to put it back. When I heard his agitated voice, "Where's my black comb? Can't anybody leave my stuff alone!," I felt a wave of panic when I saw it on my dresser. I was able to slip the comb into the top dresser drawer just before he walked into the room and asked politely if I had seen it. "No, Daddy, I didn't see it," I said, innocently. After he went downstairs, I quickly replaced it with great relief.

Too often a similar dynamic occurs in couples: the anxiety of the compulsive person spills over onto his mate, who tiptoes around to avoid setting him off. Or, on occasion, we use the delicious power of setting someone off by doing whatever triggers his reactions.

A second way compulsions affect relationships is when the person with the compulsion blames others for his agitation. As one man said, "If I don't keep the kitchen counter completely clean, she blames me for her anxiety and says, 'If you'd just pick up after yourself, I wouldn't get so upset.' " *On the spiritual path, we don't ask the world to change for us, we reflect on our own attachments.*

A third way compulsions affect relationships is that in our trance state, we aren't present for our partner or children. This is a complaint I often hear in couples: "He's off somewhere and I can't reach him."

A final way compulsions create separation is that our demanding standards prevent us from having pleasure with our partner and family. Julie commented, "When we go out to work in the yard, he's so concerned that the leaves be raked perfectly it's no fun. It ends up with criticism and hurt feelings." "She's so busy keeping the house clean or giving me lists of things to do, we can never just relax and have fun." "He always expects the kids to be quiet when he gets home and starts shouting at them for bothering him or making a mess in their rooms. I ask him to be more understanding but he just won't understand that it's his problem, not the kids'—the mess doesn't bother them." All these seemingly small compulsions add up to erode a couple's sense of union and shared commitment.

There are three primary choices you have for dealing with your compulsions:

1. Justify your compulsion on the grounds that it's important, right, better, and so on. Convince everyone around you to adjust to your compulsion. Obviously, this makes for the greatest level of separation.

2. Admit that you have a compulsion and work together as a couple to navigate around it. This is a middle ground of handling compulsions, because you have added the important dimension of awareness. If you can own up to your compulsions and not expect others to conform to your expectations, you ease the relationship. As a couple, you can discuss ways to manage it so no one gets blamed or shamed.

3. Delve beneath the compulsion and get at the underlying feelings. Notice what you experience if you don't give in to a compulsion. This would be the Buddhist approach because compulsions are forms of attachments. We can use them as a way of waking up to what's going on inside us. Remember, compulsions are always a cover for underlying feelings. Sometimes, there is a chemical imbalance in the brain that responds to medications, but in my work with trauma and neglect, I have routinely seen compulsions ease when people clear out trauma from the past. They don't need the compulsion to submerge their painful memories and feelings.

As the partner of a person with a compulsive behavior, you also have choices: while you want to be understanding, it's usually not wise to mold yourself around your partner's compulsion, which allows your partner to stay comfortably locked into his or her driven behavior with no challenge to become more aware. A better alternative is to talk with your partner: "I know you like it to be quiet when you come home, but I'm not willing to always shush up the kids." "I don't want to spend all morning Saturday cleaning, I want to go out and have some fun." "I'm not willing to have sex unless we feel connected and close."

If your partner has a compulsion he or she is not willing to explore or give up, your challenge is to allow it to be, unless you see it as a cause to end your relationship. Once you talk about its effect on you and say you'd like to see it change, it's time to step back and accept it. You don't have to like it or accommodate it, but it's time for lovingkindness and patience.

As much as possible, acknowledge compulsions, and then focus on the ways you *do* enjoy being together. When there's love and connection in a myriad of ways, that heap of papers left on the table is just a little stack of pulp. Irritating perhaps, but not a cause for battle. When there's hostility and emptiness in a relationship, the paper stack weighs a hundred pounds. When we come to the end of our days, the little things will seem so unimportant compared with how well we've loved, laughed, and treasured our lives and loved ones.

21 EXPLORE MEDITATION AND PSYCHOTHERAPY

Meditation is not something apart from life. When you are driving a car or sitting in a bus, when you are chatting aimlessly, when you are walking by yourself in a wood, or watching a butterfly being carried along by the wind—to be choicelessly aware of all that is part of meditation.

—J. Krishnamurti

The more we clear our minds of conditioning, entrenched beliefs, and expectations, the more we exist in the moment. This allows us to enter the flow of true relationship. So how does meditation, a practice central to all forms of Buddhism, relate to our discussion of relationships?

Before exploring this question, let me say that I interviewed numerous couples who have never done a sitting meditation and have had long-lasting, thriving relationships. At the other end of the spectrum, I have seen numerous people who have meditated regularly, spent years in ashrams, studied with Indian gurus, attended endless workshops, read countless books on spirituality, and even become "spiritual teachers," who have a long history of painful, unstable relationships. Why?

Relationship problems usually reflect developmental lags and stuck places from childhood that make it difficult to flow comfortably between closeness and separateness or embrace both states simultaneously. We become frozen in childhood fears, needs, and images, and often project them onto our partner. We come close, we run away. Instead of taking responsibility for our internal experience, we blame and try to change our partner. Sometimes we resort to alcohol, other drugs, and sex. Such developmental problems are primarily psychological and, I believe, best met with a psychological approach.

Throughout my twenty-seven-year experience as a psychotherapist, I have repeatedly seen people unsuccessfully trying to improve their relationships, overcome depression, cease addictions, or assuage the pain of incest and abuse with meditation, martial arts, and spiritual practices. I've seen people with black belts in various martial arts who would disintegrate into a childlike state of fear when criticized by their partner. I've seen people who have meditated for years be totally unaware of the myriad ways they are controlling and afraid. Meditation does not teach us assertiveness skills, nonviolent communication, specifically help us through developmental tasks, or directly heal sexual trauma.

Meditation was intended initially to help dissolve the mind's attachment to self, and allow people to experience their essential beingness and unity with *all that is*. Sitting meditation, over a long period of time, *can* help us become observers of our mind and slow down our reactions. But it's not the only way. Stillness and quiet and being completely present in the moment *is* meditation. It happens any time we bring our focus completely to whatever we are doing and immerse ourselves in the present without ego or an agenda—sitting quietly, chopping veggies, walking, writing, carpentry, swimming, playing music, singing to a child, or shovelling snow.

The problem with much of what is currently taught as meditation is that it is goal oriented and thus solidifies our identification with self and keeps our mind pointed toward the future. We meditate to reduce stress, to lower our blood pressure, to feel bliss, or explore our psyche. We might include an affirmation or a mantra in a foreign language that will ensure some kind of result. It sometimes becomes an isolated practice we separate from daily living. True meditation is about acceptance of whatever is happening in the moment.

Ram Tzu writes in his marvelous book, *No Way: A Guide for the Spiritually 'Advanced'*:

> *The more you pursue it*
> *The further away it goes . . .*

It is only when we give up seeking solutions, or trying to get somewhere, that we drop back into the stillness of this moment—the silence of beginner's mind—where we exist without thought, expectations, and images.

I prefer to think of meditation in Krishnamurti's words as being choicelessly aware of whatever is happening in the present. We aren't analyzing, comparing, or trying to figure anything out. We can bring this same awareness into our relationships by just tuning in to our experience. An empty mind frees us to create a living connection between us and the wondrous universe around us. We don't *do* anything to make it happen—it happens and it doesn't happen. If we're making an effort to step beyond our ego and be aware, we are caught in our ego and *trying* to be where we aren't. There is nothing to do but simply give up and choicelessly watch the butterfly being carried by the wind.

Now, to complicate this discussion with a psychological perspective. For twenty-seven years, I've been a therapist working primarily with post-traumatic stress symptoms from profound abuse, neglect, torture, and so on. While it's nice to talk about being completely present or letting go, the problem for many people is that their mind just won't quiet down. There are too many fears, emotions, and images from the past hardwired into the nervous system that constantly erupt in spite of repeated attempts to stop them or embrace them.

To reexperience them is to be retraumatized. Meditation practices often suggest that if you sit with the emotions that arise, they will dissipate. This does not always apply when there has been severe trauma. The pain or terror is simply too much to bear and the system becomes overwhelmed or the person disassociates—just as they did during the original trauma. That's where psychotherapy can be a tremendous help to clear our past trauma.

I'm not suggesting that *all* psychotherapy and counseling will help significantly. Most traditional talk therapy will *not* alleviate our hardwired reactions, because it doesn't access the nervous system and the part of the brain that holds the trauma. Moreover, traditional talk therapy often reinforces people's story line, and leads them to identify with their conditioned mind, rather than realizing that beneath their psychological concerns, they are the essence of beingness. The point of psychotherapy is to clear out the habituated reactions, relieve suffering, and create space to allow consciousness to enter. Psychological approaches using EMDR, ego-state therapy, and hypnosis can often ease those troublesome habituated automatic responses in a matter of months. (See Resources, for references and a description.)

Interestingly, a psychological approach often leads toward the clarity people seek in meditation. As we clear out trauma and our associated interpretations—that we're unlovable, undeserving, worthless, and the world is unsafe—we increasingly have an uncluttered, open mind that allows us to see others in the present, without projecting a residue of fear, hurt, and sadness from childhood. We develop a kind of receptive attention—free of effort, judgment, and striving.

Whether we are sitting, drinking tea, watching the sunrise, doing yoga, digging in a garden, or playing the piano, ultimately all that matters is to be in that river of spirit that frees us to bring a silent, living, breathing presence to all we do.

> Wherever we are is meditation.
> There is no entry and no exit . . .
> It is life moving of its own accord,
> fluid, quiet, beautiful and self-fulfilled.
> —Steven Harrison,
> GETTING TO WHERE YOU ARE

PART FIVE

WHEN I WAS A CHILD, I SPOKE AS A CHILD: AM I STILL DOING IT NOW?

22 ASK YOURSELF, "WHAT AGE AM I AT THIS MOMENT?"

We are all a marvelous maze of different parts and levels of development. A question I have found very helpful for myself and my clients is simply this: How old do I feel right now? Sometimes, we feel centered and grown-up; other times, we feel young, off-center, or confused. Our frustration might feel like a three-year-old having a tantrum, or resemble a rebellious teenager.

These states may switch rapidly in response to different people and situations. The point is to realize when we're in a childlike state and understand that it is not primarily about the current situation. We are emotionally wired into a past experience that is affecting our response. We need to stop and reflect before acting.

This is particularly useful when we have a sudden shift in mood or feel an intense surge of fear, hurt, anger, or sadness. When people ask themselves how old they feel, nearly everyone has an age come to mind, and sometimes they have a memory of a situation from the past. By asking how old we are feeling, we bring a witness or observer on board and gain an important sense of perspective: part of us is now observing our reaction instead of being engulfed by it. This split-second break in our reaction opens up the possibility of making choices about how we respond.

These sudden sojourns into the past are sometimes called an "age regression." People commonly refer to them as "being triggered," or we might say that someone "pushes our buttons." It might be that about 80 percent of our reaction comes from a back-log of feelings, and about 20 percent is actually relevant to the current situation. Sometimes it's zero percent about the current moment. Any given response might elicit a different age for different people. Feeling stubborn and defiant might feel like being a three-year-old to one person and a fourteen-year-old to another. The point is to realize when you are not reacting in current time.

While acting out of the past prevents couples from being in the "us" place, naming our reaction and taking responsibility for it brings us into connection with our partner. When I can say, "Oops, I'm feeling like a demanding three-year-old," I'm no longer reacting *as* a three-year-old. I'm observing myself, and letting my partner know what's going on with me. As couples learn to name their child states to their partner, they start to see a certain humor in the whole situation. It's astounding for most people to realize how much of the time they are reacting out of the past and not really seeing their partner in the present.

I have included some lists that reflect child states, or automatic reactions from past trauma. The idea is *not* to judge yourself or attempt some impossible notion of perfection. It's to bring awareness and understanding to yourself. For example, if you repeatedly feel worried about people's reactions—Do they like me? Am I doing it right?—it can be very helpful to understand that it is probably more about your reaction as a child to a critical parent than current reality. You can learn to say to yourself, "That was then, this is now." What is actually going on right now?

When you go through the list, explore the nature of your responses. For example, if you tend to break agreements, is it because you overcommit and feel afraid to say no, or is it because you feel resentful at being asked to help? Most of us have a few predominant age regressions. Remember, all of these responses are about conditioning. You existed before taking on all these thoughts and beliefs and your true essence or consciousness that dwells within your center is perfect and free.

Common Traits of Child States or Trauma

Fear of saying what you feel, need, think, and want.

Fear of saying no and setting limits.

Feeling hurt, mad, or rejected when someone says no to you.

Fear of being left, hurt, abandoned.

Fear of conflict and differences.

Fear of being swallowed up and losing your identity

Fear of violence. (In some cases, there is imminent danger of physical harm, in which case the fear is triggered by reality. In most cases, however, our fear is triggered by a misperception of the present moment.)

Intense angry outbursts: screaming, yelling, name-calling.

Rationalizing/making up excuses for your partner's behavior. (Well, nobody's perfect. I'm probably making too big a deal, others have it worse.)

Taking on the worries and anxieties of your partner. (Your partner is upset, so you immediately feel upset.)

Breaking agreements, not following through on tasks you agreed to do.

Blame; not taking responsibility for your actions. (I'm too tired, it's raining, you didn't remind me, fate is against me, and on and on.)

Feeling entitled to be waited on, supported, taken care of. In what ways?

Withholding, withdrawing, refusing to talk

Feeling uneasy, possessive, or jealous when your partner
seeks out new friends and feels passionate about
their interests.

Feeling afraid or embarrassed to tell your partner you've
made a mistake.

Feeling needy, insecure, or afraid of being alone.

Keeping secrets from your partner.

Defensiveness—having difficulty listening to your partner
without interrupting to explain yourself or prove your
partner wrong.

Fear of going for help when you are in serious trouble as
a couple.

Being in unequal roles, such as parent-child, teacher-
student, or enlightened one–neophyte, rescuer-
rescuee, healthy one–emotionally damaged one.

Active addictions to drugs, food, gambling, shopping,
sex, work, that are not being addressed.

Using sex to try to create a closeness that is lacking in
the relationship, or saying yes when you really want to
say no or no when you really want to say yes.

Frequent headaches, stomachaches, tensions, low energy, boredom with life, feeling stuck.

Some of the Language That Typifies Child States

"I'm afraid to tell you because I'm worried what you'll say."

"You're picking on me."

"I can never do it right."

"I never get a chance to talk."

"I'm afraid of being abandoned or rejected."

> "I can't believe people would be so dishonest, mean, inconsiderate."
>
> "I can't do this because I'm afraid."
>
> "I'm afraid to hurt their feelings."
>
> "I'm only as happy as my partner [or children] are happy."
>
> "Maybe if I'm sweeter, smarter, quieter, richer, thinner, he or she will . . ."
>
> "If you don't do what I want it means you don't love me."

To loosen the grip of these child-state reactions, stand back and observe them: "Aha, there I go feeling flooded by old hurts." "Wow, that's a hot flash of anger!" "I feel so little and scared." "How old am I?" "What was really said?" Then focus on the feelings in your body. Whatever comes, notice it, observe it, and feel it completely. This may help these entrenched reactions start to lose their grip.

The following example shows the physical and emotional responses that often signal that we are reacting out of the past.

Kay, an energetic, fun-loving woman, talked about the early years of her marriage when she was repeatedly hurt and disappointed because her husband, Jim, rarely showed up on time for dinner, nor did he call to say he'd be late. She said, "I'd feel excited and happy while cooking and imagining us together having a cozy, romantic dinner. But as it got later and later, I would feel a slow burn rising inside from my stomach to my throat. I'd think, 'How could he do that? If he loved me, how could he be so inconsiderate?' After feeling angry for a while, I'd start to feel empty and depressed. It was awful.

"Then, one day, I had this sudden thought: 'I'm not a child

anymore. I don't have to work so hard to please someone who doesn't even notice. I'm going to start eating out and seeing my friends.' "

I asked Kay what helped her make the shift. She laughed. "He was acting just like my mother, and I was acting just like I did as a kid. My mother was always disappearing one way or another—emotionally, physically—every way. So I'd keep trying to please her and it never worked. I'm not saying Jim was justified in being late, but I *was* reacting like a child."

What's so fascinating in her story is that her reactions of hurt and anger superficially appear to be a reasonable response to Jim's lack of consideration. Many people would say, "It's natural to be mad when someone is late." However, when our reaction is intense and we get stuck on a treadmill, repeating the same thing over and over, we are definitely in the past.

Her shift in behavior paid off. When Jim came home to an empty house with no dinner waiting, he was shaken out of his complacency. Kay would show up later, bright and cheery, and ask him about his day or tell him what fun she'd had visiting friends. When he finally asked, "Why aren't you cooking dinner?," she smiled and responded wisely, "Why do you think?," which left him to reflect on his behavior. After that, he phoned when he would be late, which became much less frequent, and much to Kay's delight, he even thanked her for cooking.

What this story underscores is that by recognizing that we are reacting from a child state, we can shift our focus and do something different. In doing so, we can change the balance of our relationship. Very often, it is extremely effective to follow Kay's example, and take silent action that speaks for itself.

23 FIND OUT WHO MARRIED WHOM

When couples come for counseling, I usually ask how they met, what attracted them to each other, and what were their hopes and expectations. Along with hearing a fascinating story, I'm attempting to ascertain the developmental stage of the partners when they committed to each other. In other words, were they motivated by frozen needs from early childhood that led to unrealistic expectations? Did they expect the relationship to fill them up, bring financial security, keep them from facing fears of being alone? Did they fear that no one else would ever want them, or were they desperate to get away from combative families?

In other words, were they motivated by emotional needs and fears that could never be met in a relationship, and what kind of shadow does this still cast over the relationship? While we all have various hopes and dreams when we commit to a relationship—some more realistic than others—some people are *primarily* motivated by needs that hark back to uncompleted tasks from childhood.

Not all people who marry from these ego states stay frozen in them. With self-reflection and effort, some couples are able to emerge from these confines and evolve to more adult ways of relating. On the other hand, if these frozen childlike states are not revealed, explored, and healed, they may continue to permeate the relationship in the form of clinging, withdrawal, criticism, fear, anger, or emotional distancing.

No matter how much our partner cares, he or she can never fill in the gaps left from childhood. Such expectations lead to both fear and anger. Fear that we'll always feel an emptiness, and anger that our partner is not giving us what we want. We are having a relationship with our projected images of parents or feared authority figures rather than this person we call our partner. To form a truly loving relationship in the "us" place, we need to meet each other as peers, not as children or surrogate parents.

An example: Marge and Rudy were brought up in Catholic families, well schooled in being generous, giving to others, and not "being selfish." In learning to be obedient, neither one had learned to trust his or her own feelings or observations. When they met as volunteers at a homeless shelter, Marge had finished college and was living at home while trying to find work. The home scene was contentious and Marge was desperate to get away. She had known Rudy for some time and, while she liked him, she was afraid of his temper, coupled with his drinking bouts, and tendency to withdraw and become sullen. Her mistaken thought—an extremely common one—was that her love would change him. Rudy, who was quiet and withdrawn, was attracted to Marge's bright spirit, as well as her obvious interest in him, which helped him feel needed and valued. In other words, they were both in childlike states, looking to each other to fill in the gaps. Their attraction was based on needs and fears.

Twenty years later, when they came for counseling, her comments were laced with phrases such as: "I was trying to be nice." "I thought if I was just patient longer he would . . ." Her acting-nice behavior alternated with rageful outbreaks and near-hysterical crying. There was little in between. I would point out that *trying* to be something indicates that we're feeling the opposite. In other words, if I'm *trying* to be nice, it's because I'm *not* feeling nice. I'm feeling angry, frustrated, or whatever. I suggested that if each one of them could reach deeper and say what was really going on, it would prevent the binges of anger, and withdrawal. This required working with them separately to unravel the pervasive fear and anger that had been building since childhood.

As Marge said after several months of deep psychotherapy, "I feel as if I'm coming out of a trance, like a balloon popped, and I'm seeing that I've been acting like a little girl and looking to Rudy as this man who will rescue me"— she paused and laughed—"and that sure is a ridiculous thing to do. He's as confused as I am."

If you are having difficulties in your relationship, trace back to the time you met, and review the situation for both of you. Were there shadows around your relationship of unexpressed expectations, fears, and worries? Are they still there? Did you make internal compromises and hope things would change? Were there red flags you ignored that are still posing problems in the relationship? How are you being controlled by fear right now? Then take a heartfelt look at your relationship and talk about what might help to bring you out of the past.

24 RECOGNIZE THE VALUE OF "LEAVING HOME"

Our capacity for intimacy is directly connected to our ability to maintain a sense of self *and* be in close relationship with other people. This process involves shifting our primary loyalty ties from our father and mother (or caregivers) to our new partner and family. To use Maggie Scarf's expression, we cease being in the "thrall" of our original family—their beliefs, values, and needs. We transform the relationship with our parents from being a child in need of parental approval to being equal adults—able to freely voice our feelings and opinions without fearing the reaction of our parents or caregivers. This rite of passage involves becoming aware of the values they imparted to us, and through a process of reflection and experimentation choosing which ones we want to keep, and letting go of the rest. In other words, we "leave home." In psychological terms, this is referred to as "differentiation."

Leaving home is a long-term process that starts in infancy. From the safety of our mother's arms, we slowly started to experience the world around us. If our parents were comfortable with closeness and separateness, they provided a safe haven of comfort *and* gave encouragement to forage into the world—finding new friends, learning from our mistakes, and developing passions of our own.

Differentiation is about bringing meaning into our lives and allowing our talents and interests to flourish. We develop an internal steadiness even in the face of hardships, obstacles, and people with different beliefs.

Sometimes our attempts to separate from our parents include a move across the country and a change in our lifestyle. But being reactive is still a form of being tied to our family, although it gives us room to explore ourselves and is often an important first step. The most challenging part of leaving home is recognizing the voices of our parents that live in our heads—the voices of criticism, unhappiness, fear, and shame that often dominate our internal experience. We are still fused to our parents when our ability to think, feel, and respond from our internal center is submerged beneath their messages.

If we can remember that all these voices in our heads were superimposed on our essence, we might be less afraid to take them out of hiding and look at them. While they affect us, they are not who we are. At the same time, because these voices are a hindrance to closeness, we need to stop giving them so much power over our lives.

Eventually, the loyalty to the original family's rules and demands shifts to the new family. But sometimes it's a struggle. A common complaint was voiced by Angela, who repeatedly got into a conflict with her husband, Tim, about visiting his mother's home: "When we go there, it's as if he disappears from me. He's like a little boy wanting his parent's approval. The house is like a showcase and when his mother constantly criticizes our children for touching her things, he won't stand up to her. He tells me it's my job to talk to her, but I think he should support me. I feel as if I don't have a husband and the children don't have a father when we're there." If Tim can transform his relationship with his mother by giving up his need for approval and standing beside his wife and children, he will be more able to truly come into a peer relationship with his wife. Until we leave home, we are only partially married to our partner.

The key to transformation is to bring kindness, understanding, and compassion to the parts of us that feel so confused or shameful. When we hear ourselves snapping and criticizing just as our father did, we need to go inside, be with it, and realize it's just the voice of our father living in our head. As a result, we can start dropping beneath these troublesome voices, resonate with our center, and ask, What's true for me? How do I feel? What can I do to experience the "us" place with my partner?

As we are less and less controlled by the voices from the past, we can truly marry our partner and become as one. As you can see, differentiation is just another word for someone on the spiritual path—someone who is learning to see clearly in the present and is no longer locked into automatic, habituated reactions to people and situations.

25 EXPLORE LEVELS OF RELATIONSHIPS

We have talked about the need for individuals to "leave home" in order to form an intimate relationship. Now we'll look at a series of stages that reflects our journey of leaving home. Before going through our levels of relating, I've listed some of the traits that emerge as we come into a rich and full relationship with another. Remember, it's a process—these traits are not fixed.

As we differentiate, there is an increase in the following:

- Taking pleasure and feeling at ease spending time together
- Expressing emotions and feelings and needs openly
- Listening carefully to each other with the intent of understanding
- Owning up to your mistakes without feeling ashamed
- Following through on agreements
- Considering the impact of one's behavior on one's partner
- Encouraging and supporting one's partner to become his or her best self
- An increasing ability to maintain one's identity *and* be close to one's partner simultaneously
- Working together as a team
- Ability to feel and express conflicting parts of oneself: desire to be close *and* separate, passive and assertive and so on

- The ability to apologize and forgive
- The ability to clear the air and let go
- Taking responsibility to contribute to the relationship without being asked
- An experience of union and being in the "us" place
- Humor, affection, warmth
- The ability to make a heartfelt commitment to a relationship

As people differentiate, the following traits decrease:

- Predictable, repeated conflicts between the partners
- Fear of doing it right, saying it right, being criticized, and so on
- Regarding one's partner as an object there to fulfill one's needs
- Compliance/defiance—being "good" to please the partner when she or he threatens to leave, and being defiant about taking responsibility to be a full partner in the relationship
- Self-centered behavior at the expense of the partner
- Addictive use of alcohol, food, other drugs, use of pornography
- Sex to fulfill a need or for a high
- Triangulating with children against the other parent
- Criticism, nagging, withdrawal, blaming, angry outbursts
- Feeling stuck: sense of inner powerlessness, alienation, or loneliness

As you reflect on these lists, you may remember other relationships from your life. You may notice changes you have made as well as areas where you still get stuck. Other than a few enlightened ones, none of us is always in an adult state. It's all a matter of degree, of observing and enjoying the dance, no matter where you are.

A Few Words About Stages

The ego tends to compare, rate, or grasp on to fixed ideas in order to create an identity—I'm a this or a that. So, remember, the levels I describe are just a creation of the mind. They provide a theoretical framework for your observation and reflection. Notice what your mind does as you observe and reflect. And remember, once again, we are not our behaviors. They are the surface level of our being, important, but not our essential essence, which always flows like groundwater beneath the surface.

The five levels of relating I'll talk about are based on teaching by Stuart Johnson, former director of family therapy at the Yale Psychiatric Institute, and explored with great insight by Maggie Scarf in *Intimate Partners*. I have found Johnson's framework and Scarf's exploration useful in my work with couples, and my understanding of developmental tasks in relationships. I bring my own observations and add a spiritual dimension to this exploration of evolving levels of relationships. The fundamental evolution in these stages is the ability to be comfortable being close *and* being separate.

26 LEVEL ONE: AFRAID TO BE CLOSE, AFRAID TO BE SEPARATE

At this level, being either close or separate feels equally threatening to the self. As a person approaches relationship, she or he is overcome with a fear of being swallowed up or losing one's sense of self. People say things such as: "I'm afraid I'll do it wrong, they'll always leave me, they won't like me, I'll turn into a chameleon." There is little concept of pleasure and comfort in a relationship, although there is a longing for closeness. At the other end of the spectrum, being alone feels empty or carries a terror of being cast into a void or an unending abyss.

This results in highly tumultuous relationships. There is no safety anywhere, only an unending cycle of attempting to be close, experiencing anxiety, pulling away and then feeling the terror of being alone, and trying to be close again. This reflects the most profound level of frozen child states, often stemming from early childhood disruptions in attachment and childhood neglect, abuse, or mental illness.

What can be done? People experiencing such profound fear, lack of trust, and ambivalence usually need psychotherapy to help heal the deep levels of discomfort with both closeness and separateness before they attempt to have an intimate relationship. The task is to start by being around people, developing friendships, being in supportive groups, having fun with others, learning to feel spontaneous and trusting, and then moving toward intimate relationships.

27 LEVEL TWO: SOMETIMES I SEE YOU, SOMETIMES I DON'T

What is fought out between the mates, at level two, is the problem that neither one of them has been able to address internally—the problem of how to be a distinct and separate individual while remaining emotionally attached to another human being. The core issue for these couples is each mate's inability to contain, internally, both sides of the autonomy/ intimacy polarity.

—*Maggie Scarf,* INTIMATE PARTNERS

At this stage—called "projective identification" by Johnson and Scarf—there is the potential for relationship, although the needs for closeness and separateness are still in conflict because each partner is internally aware of only one of these human needs. In other words, one person is conscious of a desire for closeness and the other is conscious of a need for distance or separateness.

In reality, the one appearing to want distance has disowned a need for closeness and the one appearing to want closeness has disowned a need to have more of a separate self. Thus, the surface conflict turns into the familiar pursuer-distancer type of relationship. It's an intricate dance of coming close, but not too close, and pulling away, but not too far away. *What needs to happen for the couple to have a more complete relationship is for each one to become internally conscious of a need for both closeness and distance.*

When we operate primarily from this stage, we have not completed our process of leaving home. Our fear of closeness or separateness usually lies in unconscious decisions we made in childhood: it's unsafe to trust anyone; if I get close, I'll get hurt; people will always leave; I don't deserve to be loved; I hurt my parents by being true to myself. We take these thoughts as "the truth" and our actions reflect these beliefs. These underlying unconscious beliefs are often the source of our behavior. Thus, we set up situations in which our greatest fears are proven true.

Relationships at this level often appear polarized. It's as if an unconscious agreement is made whereby one person carries the anger for both, while the other carries the sadness for both. Couples will fall into opposite roles of parent-child, hysterical-silent, responsible-careless, competent-incompetent, angry-sweet, depressed-cheerful, and so on. Thus, one person will appear to be hostile and the other will appear to be sweet and perpetually nice. In reality, the person who appears sweet and mellow often has buried anger that she unconsciously gets her partner to feel, and the person who explodes with anger has a kinder, more vulnerable side that has been disowned.

Another common polarity Scarf mentions is a person who has internalized and subsequently disowned an extremely distraught, crazy parent figure. As a result, he becomes adept at projecting this disordered, irrational part onto his partner, who unconsciously agrees to carry the craziness for two. Thus, the polarity widens as he appears more and more competent and sane, while she feels increasingly disoriented and unable to function. Often the person who appears to be sane leaves the relationship only to repeat the pattern with someone else.

When such a person comes for counseling, he will often say, "I have this pattern of picking crazy women." What he doesn't realize is that he has disowned a distraught, incoherent part of himself, and is picking partners that will act it out for him. If he starts dating someone who will not take on his craziness, he will feel uncomfortable and leave. Unfortunately, friends and therapists alike often respond only to the surface picture and bestow sympathy and accolades for surviving with such difficult partners. They don't help the "sane" one realize that he is dependent on his partner to carry his distraught, unorganized feelings. What we all need to remember is that as adults we choose our partner and we stay. We need to reflect on ourselves and ask, What was my part in all this?

Relationships at this level are often predictable and feel stuck. As one woman said, "I would fall into this little place. I hated it, I didn't want to be there, but I just couldn't get out."

At this level, people often feel they have to perform to be loved. This results in internal compromises and taking on the role of mother or father: "Did you remember your raincoat?" "Did you eat?" While these could be friendly gestures, more often they are an unconscious way of infantilizing ones partner so we can feel needed or important. Depression, anxiety, illness, physical symptoms, affairs, chaos, and addictions are often part of the picture.

When we're operating at this level, it's very hard to see our part in a problem, because we've so thoroughly disowned it. Because we are disconnected from so much of ourself, we often feel empty or lament that life feels bland. Put in a Buddhist context, we are lacking internal awareness. We believe that something external will fill us up, rather than realizing that the emptiness persists because we are so unaware of our inner world.

One might ask how these couples come together. We are initially attracted to someone with our disowned traits because it gives us a feeling of completion. I disown my angry side, so I feel drawn to you because you readily express anger. You fill in my missing pieces. This comfort is short-lived, however, because the very trait that I found so appealing becomes a constant reminder of that which I've disowned inside. The assertive, powerful man is now seen as domineering and insensitive. The gorgeous, flirtatious, beautiful wife is now seen as dependent, selfish, and uninteresting.

At this level, we are often confronting our partner and rarely confronting ourselves. For example, Harry disowns his internal sense of worthlessness, and repeatedly doesn't pitch in with household tasks, breaks agreements, and pressures his wife, Martha, for sex. In doing so, he sets up his partner, Martha, to be the voice of the critic, instead of facing the critic within himself. If she accepts the projection and takes on the role of critic, he then projects his self-criticism onto her by calling her a nag. Thus, he keeps the fight *externalized* between himself and his partner, rather than facing the internal discomfort of realizing how inadequate and worthless he feels.

Conversely, Harry's withholding serves a purpose for Martha— her self-definition of never getting what she wants is reinforced and she maintains her need for distance without having to own it. She can scorn him for being so dependent while she overlooks the fact that she remains in the role of nag and critic when it does not result in positive change. Often, both are afraid of seeking counseling because there is so much unconscious material inside they would have to face.

If Martha takes action and refuses to be the critic, the system will be forced to shift. If Harry can face his internal critic and feelings of inadequacy, the conflict in the relationship will diminish, although the discomfort within him will temporarily increase. *It is our willingness to bear our own internal discomfort and struggles that is key to making change.* It also makes us more sensitive and multidimensional as a human being. We become able to see the many sides of a picture or situation, just as we are aware of the many facets of our feelings and emotional states.

While relationships centered in level two are difficult, people can and do move out of them if they are willing to make the effort.

What You Can Do

1. Listen to the voices of fear in your head that prevent closeness, and realize they are learned ideas. They are not "the truth." You existed prior to taking on these ideas. Observe them, be fascinated by them, and ask yourself, What's really true for *me*?

2. Observe your behavior. What sets you off? What age levels do you fall into? What fears are controlling you?

3. Assess old loyalty ties to your parents. What would it take to truly leave your father and mother and marry your partner?

4. Stop rescuing and parenting your partner. Let him or her feel the consequences of his or her own behavior. Stop rationalizing or making excuses for your partner.

5. Keep tuning into your feelings, and peeling them back and looking underneath. Sometimes, our anger covers our sadness or our sadness covers our anger.

6. Become aware of the parts of yourself you have disowned. To start this process, look at the polarities between you and consider the possibility that you are repressing what is obvious in your partner. For example, if your partner is very needy, and you are independent, consider that you have buried a needy part of yourself. If your partner is constantly criticizing you, assume that you have an inner critic you have disowned. Remember, we get our partner to play out the part of us we don't want to see or

feel. *The more we become aware of our inner polarities, the less they are projected and played out in the relationship.*

7. Both members of the couple look at their part by asking the following questions:

- What is *my* greatest fear and what am *I* doing to make it come true?
- What is likely to happen to the relationship if nothing changes?
- What does my behavior reflect? (Dependent child, defiant little kid?)
- Once they've asked these questions, both partners can reveal to each other their own internal struggles, fears, hopes, and needs. Owning up to one's inner world is the key to moving to a less contentious, more pleasureful relationship.

8. Listening. This excercise—from Stuart Johnson—is aimed at raising awareness that the fights going on between partners are usually a substitute for facing our own painful self-accusatory beliefs. As Maggie Scarf points out, "it is psychologically easier to have our partner treat us disrespectfully than fully meet our own deep disrespect for ourselves."

The exercise. Each member of the couple takes one half hour to talk about himself or herself—their fears, joy, thoughts, interests, and experiences *separate from the relationship or the partner.* The listener is not to respond to anything that is said. This serves to block one's partner from reinforcing negative beliefs about oneself—we're unlovable, stupid, inadequate, and so on. If our partner does not speak, and we start listening to ourselves, we may start to realize that these negative beliefs actually come from within our own head. Nothing of what was said is to be discussed for at least three days, or it can be saved until seeing a counselor.

9. Trading intimacy days (also developed by Stuart Johnson). This is to help each partner have the experience of initiating intimacy. The intention is to break up the pursuer-distancer polarity.

   The exercise. On Monday, Wednesday, and Friday, one person initiates closeness. On Tuesday, Thursday, and Saturday, the other partner is given control of initiating intimacy. On a person's day, he or she makes one intimacy request that the partner has already agreed to meet (take a walk, cook together, give a back rub, and so on). Request must be specific as to action, time, and place. For example, to say, I want you to love me, be kind, be affectionate, is too vague. It must be things such as: I want to snuggle up and watch the video *Yentl* together.

10. Explore all your escape hatches in life—TV, Internet use, constant music, being busy, sugar, shopping, talking endlessly on the phone, *and especially alcohol and other drugs.* With couples at this level, there are numerous escape hatches operating because there is so much emptiness and pain. I suggest to anyone not feeling complete in their relationship to cease *all* use of alcohol and other drugs, even if you don't believe it is a problem. Then look at all the other ways you distance yourself from your internal world and your partner.

11. Both people take responsibility to join support groups and get professional help to become more self-aware and learn to embrace a wider range of emotions and feelings.

LEVEL THREE: KNOWING YOURSELF SO YOU CAN KNOW YOUR BELOVED

Partners at this level, when swept up in a marital battle, are likely to behave and even feel like level [two] couples, but eventually, when they calm down, they can acknowledge the existence of their own internal ambivalences. The key difference at level three is that even though the spouses are projecting unwanted thoughts and feelings onto one another, there is not so much unconscious process involved.
—*Maggie Scarf*, INTIMATE PARTNERS

Although couples at this stage may get entrenched in an ongoing battle, they eventually can sit back and own up to their part in creating the situation. An example from Lawrence and Marie: A fundamental agreement between them was that she was the primary breadwinner and he would take care of the home and be available when their three daughters came home from school. When Marie was preparing for her fiftieth birthday celebration in their modest home, she asked Lawrence to please clean up his bathroom and paint the garage doors to make the house nicer for their guests.

Lawrence, who was quite content with the house as it was and hated painting, initially balked and didn't follow through. A predictable fight ensued about his responsibility to do his part. To Marie's delight, when she came home from work a few days later, the bathroom was cleaned and the paint cans were sitting beside the garage. This is the departure from level two, where the bathroom would have remained uncleaned and the garage doors would have never been painted. In other words, in level three, the arguments may look the same as level two, but there is a significant difference: namely, after people cool off, they reflect on themselves, and change their behavior. They might come back and apologize, or finish up the project that has been left undone for so long.

I spoke to Lawrence about how he made the shift from stalling out to following through. It was a clear example of moving from I versus You to the "us" place: "At first I just thought to myself, I don't care if the bathroom is dirty, and I hate painting. Especially since the garage doors are rotting and it's useless. But then I realized, it's Marie's party, and I want her to have a good time. So I looked at the house through Marie's point of view, and did things as she would like them. She often gives me lists and then I do it."

For Lawrence to lead the way into level four of relating, he could come to Marie and ask, "What could I do to help with your party?" Better still, he could look around the house and make a list of what needed to be done, talk it over with Marie, and they could jointly decide on a plan.

At level three of relating, each person starts to experience the internal struggle of being true to oneself *and* being close. However, being close is sometimes experienced as a loss of being oneself. For example, if you wanted to spend the afternoon watching a sporting event on TV, you would feel torn if your partner asked you to take a walk. If you joined your partner because you wanted to create "togetherness," it might feel as if you were giving up a part of yourself as opposed to simply switching plans. This might result in feeling resentful later on.

I spoke with Rick and Joni, a couple in therapy that are in the process of making a clear shift from level two to level three after twenty-five years of marriage. He recounted an event at an airport where he had walked away in the cafeteria line to look for a table without letting her know and she had felt little and abandoned. A typical fight ensued. But they had gotten through it and felt victorious at having escaped an old pattern. It shows a distinct move from level two to level three behavior. I asked Rick for his perspective on how he handled the situation differently than before.

"Well, first we got in the same old fight. She was hurt and mad, and I felt terrible, like I was bad. It all felt like too much was happening at once and I wanted to stop the action. Then I did that male thing: I blamed her—kind of like getting in the first punch at a bar so you end the fight and you don't have to go outside and get a broken lip. But I kept asking myself, 'How old do I feel?' and there was a tiny break in that panic thought train, and I asked myself, What could I do differently? I didn't handle it well at the time. But because I'm so elated that overall we're making progress, the next morning I talked to a guy in my AA meeting. He helped me see how I'd put her down, so I dropped in at her office, and apologized." Rick had taken three important steps that opened the door to level three and beyond. He had reflected on himself, taken advice from an outside person, and apologized.

I also asked for Joni's perspective. At first, her stance was to be pleased that she finally had a grown-up for a husband because he had apologized. That was a level-two response because she was not reflecting on herself. After an in-depth therapy session, however, she was able to understand that her panic of feeling so scared when he had walked away belonged to her and had contributed to the upheaval they had experienced. She was able to go back to him that night and tell him she had felt scared and little when she looked up and he wasn't there. She was also able to request that he let her know when he was going to walk away from her. Rick agreed to her request. Then he asked with a smile, "How old were you, anyhow?"

"You're not going to hold it against me, are you?" she quipped.

"No."

"I was five."

Rick told me that later that night he looked in her and saw nothing but love. "It makes you feel so damn good. Like you can change. It doesn't always have to be the same old way. I keep learning that my perspective on a situation often isn't true at all. The truth is that we've both been confused a lot. But now we whittle away at it, keep talking about it, and I take back those sharp things I spit out. Eventually, we get down to the truth, it's always there. Then everything feels okay."

By reflecting on themselves, owning up to their experience, explaining what they were feeling, and keeping the conversation in the spirit of exploration instead of blame, they moved squarely into level three. It will no doubt be a continual crossing over the line, but with every success, it will become more natural and easy.

What You Can Do to Bring Yourself into Level Three and Beyond

1. Continue the exercises from level two.
2. Bring up your internal conflicting feelings and talk about them together. "I'd like to be with you and take a walk, but I really want to watch this tennis match on TV." Don't sacrifice your self or do something you'll resent.
3. Negotiate times for being close and times for being separate. Talk about your ambivalent feeling. Be honest.
4. When you have conflicting feelings, ask yourself, "How old am I?" and then reflect on your behavior. Ask yourself, "How would

I act if I were being an adult? How would I act as the lover and
the friend?"

5. Apologize when you blame, shame, or discount your partner.
Own up to it.

6. Continue to notice the polarities in the relationship. Keep asking yourself if you can see yourself in your partner's behavior.
An exercise is to write down everything that irritates you about
your partner and see how you have similar or parallel traits or
have done similar behaviors in the past.

Sometimes in the beginning we'll say, "No, no, I don't get
angry. It's my partner who gets angry." But then look deeper.
Do you lose your temper, put other people down, have a tight
jaw, or numerous headaches?

Then write down all that you appreciate and like in your
partner and see if you have parallel traits or behaviors as well.

7. Switch roles. Take a familiar argument and play each other's part.

8. With the intent of truly listening, ask your partner, "Am I loving
you well? Do you feel understood? What could I do to make
our relationship better?"

Reflecting again on Buddhist principles, we exert ourselves
to look deeper, go for help, and own up to our behavior. This is
truly the stuff of awakening and creating a loving relationship.
When two people join together in this process with a strong intent to do whatever it takes to improve their partnership, long-
standing stalemates can be broken and new levels of
tenderness, humor, kindness, and passion can emerge.

29 LEVEL FOUR: FEELING AT PEACE WITH CLOSENESS AND SEPARATENESS

At this level, which Johnson and Scarf call "tolerating ambivalence," each individual is more aware of the inner push-pull of his or her needs and desires. Both partners experience the conflicting needs for closeness and separateness *within* themselves and are able to voice their ambivalence or confusion. They have a greater tolerance for inner complexity and can take responsibility for their feelings because they are conscious of them.

At this level, our inner world becomes more dynamic and complex and conflicts are not two-dimensional—right-wrong, my way–your way. Rather, each person can see the situation from both sides of the relationship.

As an example: I was having dinner with my dear friends Margaret and Allan, married twenty-eight years. I asked Margaret if they would be taking a vacation that summer.

Margaret looked at her husband with a knowing smile and said, "Well, we've been struggling with this. Allan wants to go to his family reunion and wants me to come. I like his family, and would like to be with him. But I've had to ask myself, where am I in all this? What do I need in my life right now? I haven't had time to explore my creative interests because I'm working at the nursing home and there are so many needs at home. So I've decided to go to a week-long pottery workshop. I know Allan isn't happy about it, but it feels right."

Allan responded, "I'm sad she won't be coming—it's more fun

when we're together at these family things—but I do completely understand her need to do something for herself, and I will have a good time anyhow."

Her artful description of the problem includes complete awareness and acceptance of her needs for closeness and for separateness. This allowed her to come to a decision without concocting excuses that are typical at levels two and three. She acknowledged her partner's feelings with compassion, yet made a decision that felt in tune with herself. No one was wounded, rejected, or left out of her consideration, and no one was right or wrong. She was simply reflecting on her own stream of awareness and being led by it. Likewise, Allan could also maintain his desire to be with her, yet understand her need for separateness, and know he could go to the family reunion and have a good time on his own.

Paradoxically, when we accept conflicting undercurrents inside, they don't take on momentous proportions, because we regard them as natural, and sometimes fascinating. This underscores once again that our individual commitment to self-awareness is at the heart of both our spiritual journey and our ability to create intimacy in our lives.

At this level, people feel an internal steadiness and an ability to voice their needs, so that intimacy does not carry the risk of being swallowed up. Each person has a safe internal home to return to. Both partners are attentive to not treating their mate as an object to fulfill their needs. For example, having sex to fulfill an unconscious need for a sexual high would feel wrong to both of them. They wouldn't want to do this to themselves or to their partner.

Because they relinquish attachments more readily than at earlier stages, the partners are more in touch with their essential nature, and feel greater lightness and joy in their relationship.

30 LEVEL FIVE: I AND THOU—WE ARE ONE, WE ARE TWO

Do you want to know what's in my heart?
From the beginning of time, just this! just this!
                                                        —Ryokan

Here, we have reached the promised land of relationship—the milk and honey of sharing one's life with another person. We are both in love with our partner and in love with life by way of our partner. The closeness-separateness polarities that were previously problematic have dissolved. There is little or no internal conflict between being intimate and being separate because one derives pleasure and meaning in being together and being apart.

We can dissolve into our beloved—giving, sharing, and making love without holding back—because we have no fear of losing ourselves. Similarly, we can be apart without feeling lonely or afraid because we feel richly alive and the love of our partner dwells within us. At this level, both members of the couple have "left home" and are completely married to each other, which is reflected in their loyalty and their desire to please, comfort, and care for each other.

At this integrated level of relating, traits such as dependence-independence are felt and understood as natural parts of one's interior. They are not at odds with each other; rather, they both have a place, just as being separate and together have their own rhythm and harmony. Both members of the couple have access to a wide array of feelings and emotions. Each one can be sweet and strong, passionate and gentle, passive and assertive. In the fullness of their separate lives, they bring a richness to each other. It's as if they can enjoy all the seasons, finding something that pleases, something to relish, and something to look forward to.

Conflicts that arise are negotiated primarily on an external level, because there is no underlay of meaning and wondering that keeps conflict simmering at an unconscious level: Do you love me? Do I matter? Am I worthwhile? Will you stay with me? Problems are solved with complete goodwill for both oneself and one's partner. There is not a clear demarcation line between conflict and loving. As the Quakers say, everything is a meeting for worship—whether we are gathering to pray, to celebrate a marriage, to have a picnic, to solve conflicts, or to give guidance to someone in turmoil. We are always asking to live in the heart of truth, and be guided by spirit.

In Buddhist terms, we might say that each member of the couple has absorbed the meaning of kindness and compassion. It's not a behavior, it's just how one is. Level five is not a fixed state. People may slide in and out of levels four and three at times. But they are committed to seeing clearly in the present, being responsible for their feelings, and recognizing their attachments without projecting them onto their partner via blame and hostility.

Couples at this level usually stay in touch, even when one is away for a period of time. Jessie mentioned a time when Dan took their son on a vacation to Florida. I asked Jessie how often they phoned and she said, "Every day," as if it would be obvious. She continued, "You want to know what's going on, and if you call a day or two later, the excitement is gone, it's not so alive and real." Her response typified the vitality and dynamic quality of highly evolved relationships. The pleasure they derive from each other is like a river that never ends—a river they keep alive and flowing.

How People Move from One Level to Another

There are myriad ways people evolve through these levels. Sometimes, there is a moment of grace and awakening when someone says, "I don't want to live this way anymore." Women have instigated change after taking a women's study class. People gain insight from books and observing friends. Sometimes, pain and emptiness are the catalyst. Other times, people go through a time of stability and feel an inner surge of strength to be more honest in their relationship. Others get there through psychotherapy or various retreats and spiritual practices.

Sometimes, if one person moves to a higher level, it inspires their partner to follow. For example: When Paul and Haley were newly married—a third marriage for both—Haley got a notice saying that as a widow, she was entitled to receive $63.52 a month if she weren't married. She laughingly read the letter out loud to Paul, and quipped, "Well, if I had known this, I wouldn't have gotten married." Paul stormed out of the room, obviously feeling wounded. Haley waited a little while, then went to him.

"Paul, I understand that what I said hurt your feelings, and I don't want to hurt you . . . but . . . [she smiled at him] get used to it, I joke a lot." With her skillful reply, Haley acknowledged his feelings, remained centered in herself, and invited him to meet her at a higher level of differentiation. If she had felt guilty for "hurting him" and started to hold back her humor, they could have drifted back into levels three and two.

Interestingly, as Paul looked back on this incident, he said, "The greatest thing I've learned from Haley is to have a sense of humor. I was brought up in a serious family. She kept me from being such a professor all the time."

Haley laughed. "When we were first married, I used to say things like 'Do I have to pay tuition for this lecture?' " Her relentless playfulness and humor and his adoration of her took them into the flow of a wonderfully loving relationship.

Wherever you are on this map of relationships, know that through your growing awareness of your internal world, you can make dramatic shifts in your relationships. It is truly a rewarding journey, worthy of our best effort.

PART SIX

COMMUNION IS THE PURPOSE OF COMMUNICATION

31 TUNE IN TO THE DANCE OF SENDING AND RECEIVING MESSAGES

Sound . . . rhythm . . . vibration . . . words. . . .
Communication is the means whereby consciousness
extends itself from one place to another.
—*Anodea Judith,* WHEELS OF LIFE

Communication is about sending and receiving information, thoughts, ideas, and emotions. With infinite nuances, our words blend together with the rhythm, tone, depth, and quality of our voices. When we are congruent in sending messages, our eye contact, the sound of our voice, the movement of our body, and the meaning of our words are harmonious.

The foundation for listening and understanding is an open, uncluttered mind that has room to hear another. This takes us back to beginner's mind—a mind free of fear, expectations, and judgment. However, if judgments and fears arise, we can still observe them as thoughts and not identify with them or take them as truths. We can let them drift like clouds in our mind so we have room to be present to ourselves and our partners.

True listening means we tune in to the spirit behind the words. We don't critique minor inconsistencies or point out mistakes in grammar. Just as meditation is about "choiceless awareness" in the moment, we can use conversation as a form of meditation to attune to all that is being conveyed.

Conversations take on a harmony, rhythm, and counterpoint

all their own. There is a time for empathy, a time for discussion, for problem-solving, or to let off steam. When we listen to a person describe how his or her day went, we don't need to comment, except maybe to say, "Gee," "Bummer," "No kidding," or "Sounds tough." We can draw out our partner's experience by asking her questions: "How was that for you?" "What did your boss say?" If our lover or a friend calls in distress and wants us to help him sort through a problem, we might take a more active role. If he asks for advice or ideas, we can offer them up—simply and clearly. And if he starts to "yes but" what we say, we can drop back, stop making suggestions, and say, "I wish you the best."

We often open the conversation by making little contracts: "I need your input on a situation I'm troubled with. Do you have time to talk?" "Do you want to hear about my lousy day?" "Do you want to hear my good news?" "Can I tell you about my trip to the doctor?" "Can I have a few minutes to whine?"

There is no set of specific rules or no one way to converse. Communication is about communion, which means interchange and connection.

32 REMEMBER THE BASICS OF GOOD COMMUNICATION

Most people will say that good communication is at the heart of solid relationships. Unfortunately, our habituated patterns of shame and fear often block the pathways of connection. We start to listen and become defensive. Our mind wanders. We've heard it all before.

Many of us are unaware of our communication patterns or we

slip in and out of our awareness of them. We may notice irritating patterns in others, but we don't see them in ourselves. Other times, we do see our troublesome patterns but still feel unable to stop interrupting, turning the conversation back to ourselves, and so on. The following steps can aid us in becoming a more receptive listener, as well as speaking more simply.

Guidelines for Listening

1. Breathe deeply, relax your belly, and drop back a bit so you are in a receptive stance, not perched to respond. Keep focused on breathing and relaxing.

2. Listen with the intention of understanding and entering the other's world, not teaching, analyzing, fixing, interrupting, or defending yourself.

3. Note any inner desire to jump in quickly, give advice, smooth over pain, or talk about yourself. Take a breath.

4. If you want to say something, check your motivation. Is there a judgment or uneasiness behind it? Do you feel eager to quiet her worries, cheer him up, or start talking about yourself? If so, wait. Breathe. Pull back. If something arises in you that is free of judgment or intent to change the person, then say it.

5. Show that you are listening. While sometimes it's enough to listen in complete silence, it might be helpful to say, "Oh, you're really upset. What a tough situation." The person will usually give a sigh of relief because she feels listened to.

6. Notice when a conversation takes on a spontaneous, easy flow of listening and responding. Register how that feels.

7. If you need to end the conversation, you can break in and say something like: "I don't want to be rude, but I need to get back to work. I wish you the best."

8. If a conversation feels stuck or is overwhelming, you can say so. "I do want to hear what you are saying, but I'm feeling overwhelmed with so much detail." Or "I really don't want to get into a 'how bad it is' conversation. I'm aware of these things, but it doesn't feel good to me right now." In other words, we can say the truth . . . kindly.

Guidelines for Speaking

1. Breathe, relax your shoulders, and drop into your belly so your words can arise from an inner stillness. Don't speak while holding your breath. Often people take a deep breath and start talking rapidly—kind of like the windup and the pitch—as if they want to get it all out before someone stops them.
2. Remember that true connection usually comes from sharing your personal experiences.
3. Avoid excess detail. Get to the heart of your message. Extensive background information or details about other people often obscure the essence of your experience. Remember, it is usually uninteresting to talk at length about people unknown to your listener.
4. Notice the energy level of the conversation. A true connection will feel alive and flowing. If the energy drops, or you start feeling tight or blank in your chest, or the words seem flat, pull back, and tap into your experience, name what's happening, take a break, or end the conversation.
5. Allow moments of silence. Pause at the end of a couple of sentences and breathe so the other person can respond, and you can hear yourself.
6. Notice how the listener is responding. Is she restless, looking away, or tapping her fingers? This usually signifies she is not

with you and you need to pause. You could even check in: "Am I rambling?" "Do you need to be going?"

7. Recognize when it's time to end the conversation. Sometimes, we want to keep talking because we feel a nice connection with the other person. You can say that—"I really enjoy talking with you and it's hard to say good-bye"—and then end the conversation. Don't hang on.

There are some basic ways people block connection in conversation. Usually, it's when we don't stay tuned in with both the message and the feelings.

How We Block Connection

1. Taking the conversation back to yourself. As in, "I did that too." Someone says, "I'm going to be in Virginia for vacation," and the other person says, "Oh, my son lives there," and then starts talking about her son.

2. Analyzing. Person A says, "I'm so upset that Jack has taken a second job," and Person B responds, "Maybe it's because . . . " or "Do you think it's because . . ." This takes the conversation out of an emotional level into a left-brain analysis of someone who isn't even present. The listener isn't responding to the feelings of the speaker.

3. Shifting the topic to someone else: "My sister has that problem."

4. Not responding at all—looking blank, shuffling your feet, scanning the ceiling.

5. Making patronizing statements: "Everyone goes through that." "You'll be all right." "Don't be afraid, there's nothing to worry about."

6. Responding with platitudes: "God never gives you more than you can handle." "I'm sure it's an important lesson for your growth."

7. Changing the subject completely: "Oh, by the way, did you hear about the new sporting goods store about to open?"

8. Interrupting to ask for unimportant details, like dates, times, places. "How long has this been going on?" "Where did it happen?" This shifts the conversation from the essence of the experience into facts and figures, which keep us away from connection.

While it's important to weave a tapestry of connection by responding to someone, most people could slow down, listen more, and wait longer to respond. Then they can respond more fully and with a richer understanding.

If you want to change your patterns, it usually works best to take one thing you want to change and focus on it daily. This can be your mindfulness practice. For example, if you tend to include excessive detail, respond with platitudes, interrupt, or give advice, you could pick one, get a little notebook, notice your interactions throughout the day, and write down what happened. When you find yourself doing the unwanted behavior, observe it, notice your breathing, the tension in your body, and ask what you are feeling underneath. At the end of the day, sit down and recall the different situations, remember your responses, then peel each one back by going underneath and ask, "What was going on with me at the time?" "Was I trying to impress someone, defend myself, show that I'm competent, come across as a good guy?"

Don't be hard on yourself. Stay focused on one particular behavior for several months unless you feel a shift in a shorter amount of time. You might be surprised at the internal changes you feel. As you become a more receptive listener and more able to speak and respond from the stillness within, you will notice your relationships changing.

Remember, these are just guidelines drawn from observations. The context of the relationship is an important part of the equation. With close friends and intimate partners, we may break in more often, give feedback, and be more active. Every relationship—be it with a friend or lover—has its own amazing composition. In getting to know each other's ways, we become more highly attuned to making connection through conversation.

33 GIVE NO ADVICE—WELL, MOST OF THE TIME

I feel with loving compassion the problems of others without getting caught up in their problems that are giving them lessons they need for their growth.
—*Ken Keyes,*
HANDBOOK TO HIGHER CONSCIOUSNESS,
Eighth Pathway

Advice giving is often a form of quelling our own anxiety. We rush in with advice out of our own need to have everything peaceful and happy. If we accept that there's nothing inherently bad or wrong with struggle, discomfort, anxiety, or making a mistake, we will be able to be a compassionate friend and not jump in with suggestions to stop others from having their feelings.

Intimacy rests on simply being the witness to each other and entering into connection through empathy and lovingkindness. If we want equality in a relationship, if we want a genuine relationship, it's important to avoid a a one-up one-down, teacher-student, leader-follower type of connection. In general, people tend to give advice instead of revealing their personal feelings and wants.

For example, if my partner is considering a job that means extra work at night, I might try to change him to fit my agenda through coded messages: "Don't you think you'll get tired and overwhelmed if you have to work so many nights?" This is indirect and puts the focus on him, rather than me. I'm on safe ground if I say, "I feel uneasy about you taking that job if it means you will be away so many nights. I need your help with the children and I want us to have time together. I'm willing to live with less money to be with you more." This way, I stay on my side of the fence and say what's going on with me. I don't make slippery, patronizing remarks.

If you feel a powerful urge to give advice, ask permission first. For example, you might want to say, "I'm having a strong reaction to what you're saying. Do you want to hear it?" or "I have an observation about this. Is it okay if I say it?"

The reverse of offering unsolicited advice is feeling you have to accept unsolicited advice. I remember when a good friend made an announcement to all her friends: "I don't want advice from anyone. I've followed what everyone said for most of my life, and I need to listen to myself for a change." If someone gives you unwanted advice, you can respond by saying, "I appreciate your interest, but I'm just wanting someone to listen." If the other person presses you, you can say, "Advice is not helpful to me right now, I'm just needing support." Assure them that you care, but continue to set a limit.

Sometimes, if we feel a person is on a collision course, it may be appropriate to cross the line and make a strong statement that includes expressing your need: "I'm so worried when you ride your motorcycle after you drink. It feels like asking for trouble and I would hate to see you or another person get hurt. I really want you around." "I really wish you'd follow up on that suspicious mammogram. I feel panic when you dismiss it. I don't want to even think about losing you." "I'm concerned with what's happening on your new job. You come home more and more depressed and grouchy and you can't seem to say no to working overtime. I want us to have some time together, and have the energy for making love." These statements are most effective when done directly with eye-to-eye contact, and in a resonant, clear voice. Generally, once or twice is the limit, because otherwise we start pleading or sounding like a critic.

If our partner doesn't comply or do what we wish they would, we need to shift the focus to ourselves, because we can't change the other person. This can be extremely painful. When my mother had severe angina, my heart ached when I'd see her clutch her chest and grab for her nitroglycerin. I wanted her to change her diet, exercise, get bypass surgery or nutritional counseling. But it wasn't her way. She stayed with traditional medicine, often gasped in pain, gobbled nitroglycerin pills, and died much younger than she might have otherwise. But I'm glad I wasn't nagging her on our last phone call, the day before she died. Because I had let go, albeit with great sadness, our last conversation was one of love and joy. She had sung in the church choir, gone on a church picnic, and was feeling the love of those around her.

Part of giving advice rests on knowing the disposition of your partner or friend. What seems like care and concern to one will feel like an intrusion to someone else. One time, when I was visiting relatives at a summer cabin and setting off to ride the four-teen miles around the lake, my cousin said, "You shouldn't ride your bike on the highway. It's dangerous with all those trucks." When I told this to a friend, she responded, "I bet that made you mad—as if you don't know what you're doing."

"No," I responded. "I felt cared about. I've so seldom had any-one worry about me." In the dance of relationships, we're always learning the particular traits of our friend or beloved with regard to giving and receiving advice. Even then, there's no way we'll al-ways get it right. But that's okay. We just do our best and talk about the rest.

So avoid giving unsolicited advice, ask permission when you do, and if you cross the line, do it with gusto and clarity, then step down and remember that everyone has to find his or her own way. When we let go of control, we step together into silence, where truth can be heard, where we can hear the beating of our hearts together, joined in love.

34 ASK FOR NO ADVICE— EXCEPT SOMETIMES

When the Navajo child asked her mother for counsel on a particular question, her mother said, "Put it in your holy middle and sleep on it."

If you tend to look to everyone else as an expert, including your partner, you are discounting your own internal wisdom. When we seek out teachers, priests, shamans, gurus, and others to show us the way, we are assuming that there is a way. We are also reinforcing our identity of self as *not-knowing-the-answer* or *everyone-knows-more-than-I-do*. We need to realize that wisdom rests in experience, observation, and reflection that combines head and heart. It's something that arises of itself. Teachers may have something useful for us to draw on, but ultimately we need to listen to ourselves. It's better to speak from our heart, even if we are stammering and awkward, than to glibly parrot the words of others.

When trying to hear your inner guidance, you may have many voices chiming away inside that need to be sorted out: this could include, "I want to work harder," "I want more time off," "I'm scared of losing my job," "What the hell, let's have a beer." In sorting through these internal voices, you may want to also ask, "Which is the voice of a worried child? Which is the voice of wisdom—of my adult self?"

Sometimes, when we are conflicted, it's better to get out of our mind and put our question or concern in our "holy middle" and trust that the answer will come in time. Instead of trying to figure it out, we can become engaged in life—browse in a bookstore, talk with friends, go to a park, listen to the birds. When we open all our receptive senses and tune in to the world, the answers to our questions often rise to the surface quite effortlessly.

If your mind still feels like a carousel going around and around with the same thoughts, ask yourself, "What would I be feeling if I let myself know the truth about this situation?" Usually, when we are obsessing, we are avoiding knowing what we know. We don't want to face an unpleasant truth that could disrupt our lives.

How does this relate to couples? In an equal partnership, when both people have access to their internal wisdom, they can fully enter into dialogue. Instead of playing teacher-student, or parent-child, our conversations become a rich interweaving of our responses, thoughts, and feeling as they arise in the moment. It becomes a creative interplay that has a freshness and originality. We don't speak for the other, but we help throw wood on the fire of our creativity and imagination.

35 YOU CAN DEFEND YOURSELF WITHOUT BEING DEFENSIVE

At one point in my unfolding journey, I was told that I should just listen to others and not be defensive. But I confused not being defensive with not standing up for myself. If someone criticized me, I thought I should just accept what they said and not respond. The problem was, by failing to describe my reality or defend myself, I wasn't being honest or taking care of myself.

We need to be able to discern if we are jumping in with defensiveness, or if we are honoring and protecting our essential self. Some people have been conditioned to think immediately that whatever goes wrong is their fault. I remember in my women's therapy groups, if someone got mad and stormed out, I would ask the remaining group members, "Okay, so how many of you think she left because of something you did?" At least half of the hands went up, if not more. We'd usually have a good laugh as everyone revealed what she thought she had done wrong. And, of course, no one had done anything wrong. If someone storms out, she storms out. Unfortunately, when we walk around with perennial guilt stalking us, we can find a way to take the blame for almost anything. If there is a shred of truth in someone's criticism of us, we think to ourselves, Well, maybe I did do something seriously wrong. We need to find that core within us that serves as a guidepost and helps us rest securely within ourselves.

I remember my therapist practically shouting at me when I was taking the blame for something I didn't do. "Charlotte, you didn't do anything wrong! You're giving yourself away! You need to defend yourself and say what's going on for you!" I can still hear her words ringing in my head, penetrating the fog of guilt and self-doubt that kept me from speaking up for myself. I'm thankful for her willingness to be so expressive with me.

We need to be able to say things such as: "No, that wasn't my intention, that was not my perception of the situation, that's not how I experienced it." You don't need to debate with the other person, but you need to state your case. If your partner or a friend misinterprets, misquotes, or says inaccurate things about you, kindly and clearly give them your perspective.

If the current situation isn't conducive to sharing your response, you can still trust yourself. You don't need validation from anyone to trust your perception. So if someone tells you you're wrong, don't crumble and immediately think their perception is more accurate than yours. You can listen to them, but remember to come back to yourself and your holy middle. On the Buddhist path, we don't want to create separation—and that includes separation from our feelings and internal experience. When people remain silent because they are scared to speak up, they are allowing fear to control their lives.

Remember, relationships are about two growing, open, honest people coming together to help each other be their best selves. If we remain silent, and allow someone to blame us, we enable them to believe their misperception. This casts a fog over the relationship. It is important not to collude in this faulty arrangement that prevents us from being in a full relationship with each other. From the "us" place we want to know the truth and we want to understand our partner's point of view.

36 LEARN THE ART OF APOLOGY

To be human is to sometimes say I'm sorry. Even if we have no intent to harm, our behavior might be perceived as hurtful, insensitive, or mean. The bridge back to an "us" place is to acknowledge the hurt the other person feels, and to listen while they explain how our behavior has affected them. Then we can apologize and say something to show we understand: "I'm sorry. That was a thoughtless remark, and I can see how it would be hurtful." "I'm sorry I made plans without consulting you, that was wrong of me. I should have asked you first." Put the focus on your partner (or friend) by acknowledging the impact of your behavior. If you immediately pour out a litany of reasons and excuses, you are keeping the focus on yourself.

After you've apologized, it's sometimes helpful to give reasons. You were caught up in traffic, the store was closed, or you had difficulty extricating yourself from a meeting. There are legitimate reasons on occasion, but first acknowledge the inconvenience to the other person. I would also suggest avoiding the flimsy excuses that make you sound like a naughty child. Or, if you give them, do it with a sense of humor: "Do you want to hear my lame excuse?" Generally, when we are sloppy, inattentive, and careless, it's better to just say so: "I knew it was getting late, but I just kept talking on the phone, and I realize that's no excuse. I feel bad that I put you out."

An artful apology becomes real when we explore our inner world by asking ourselves, "What was my motivation? Why did I run one more errand when I knew I'd be late? Why did I get so mad and make that cutting remark? Did I intend to do harm? Have I been building up resentment? Or is it just an annoying habit?" We need to reflect on what was going on within us at the time.

When we hurt another person, we need to give something back. It's like putting our love into action. If you inconvenience your partner, or anyone, for that matter, cook a special dinner, wash extra dishes, take them to a movie, vacuum the house, or do something that gives back what you took away—namely, time and energy. This must not be done out of guilt; rather, we do it in good faith knowing that to err is human.

Going one step deeper into the art of apology, remember: it's not enough to repeatedly say you're sorry for the same hurtful behavior. That's a bit like saying a rosary before cheating on your partner. We need to be more responsible and explore why we're being so careless in our relationship, or what led us to stray so far from lovingkindness. Our commitment to change our behavior must have an internal ring to it. We aren't attempting to *do good*, we are committing ourselves to *be* fully attuned to ourselves and live by our integrity.

Shifting to another perspective for a moment: What if someone says she is hurt by us, and it feels totally unconnected to our behavior? Should we apologize if we feel we have done nothing wrong? One approach is to acknowledge the person's feelings and give our perspective: "I realize you felt hurt by what I said, and I'm very sorry about that. I had no intent to harm. I feel you are misreading my intentions."

If we have apologized and someone won't let the subject drop, we can ask, "What needs to happen so I don't keep hearing about this? I've said I'm sorry, I've acknowledged wrongdoing. I don't know what else you want from me." This may be the time for a more involved discussion about the relationship. It may also be a time for the person who won't let the subject drop to examine his or her own motivation. Why am I hanging on to this hurt and anger? Why do I keep bringing this up? Is there a stockpile of old grievances that need to be aired? Am I dwelling on my partner's mistake to give me a sense of power by making her feel guilty?

Perfectionistic people often have difficulty apologizing or asking forgiveness because it reveals their imperfections, which they experience as shameful. But, remember, when you get defensive and start blaming rather than apologizing, you're implicitly telling yourself you have something to be ashamed of.

Now to talk about being on the receiving end of an apology. When someone offers a heartfelt apology, we do well to listen and do our utmost to accept it. Otherwise, the rupture lives on within us and between us. We might feel so relieved and blessed by an apology that we can easily let the matter go. Sometimes, we still bear resentments and need to talk further or explore why we're still holding on. *It's important to be clear with ourselves, because accepting an apology means putting the whole subject to rest and not bringing it up again.*

It's important to remember that it is never too late to make amends. When we give and receive forgiveness, we open that tender spot in our hearts and become a source of healing for ourselves and others.

37 REBUILD THE BRIDGE: FORGIVENESS AND LETTING GO

Forgiveness is about releasing our resentments, pain, and desire for retribution against another. It's like saying, I see you as human, I do not bear judgment against you, and I hold no claim on account. We become able to forgive when we can step back and see the other person doing what they are conditioned to do. We may not like what they did, and even see it as mean and cruel. Yet, if we can fully grasp the Buddhist principle that hurtful behavior stems from ignorance, pain, and suffering, we may eventually feel mercy and compassion instead of anger and judgment. But it's not always easy.

When we feel the shock of being hurt by someone we love, we reel with thoughts such as: How could someone I love do that to me? What have I done wrong? We may feel bleak and empty or want to retaliate and counterattack. Our survival mechanism is triggered to self-protect, to shut down.

The heart of forgiveness is loving compassion for our imperfect selves. As Buddhist teacher Pema Chodron explains, if everything is Buddha nature, then we're Buddha being angry, Buddha losing our temper, Buddha dissolving into fear. We can't escape from our Buddha nature, because it's contained in all our actions. It's everything. If I have made friends with my fear, my impatience, my hurt, or desire to make someone feel guilty, then I will feel acceptance when others do the same. When I see through the eyes of understanding and compassion, I can forgive. I see your storm clouds, your lightning, and still remember your sunshine. We can keep reminding ourselves that people are just doing what they are conditioned to do, and that it's not a reflection of ourselves.

In the Jewish tradition, the Rosh Hashanah holiday addresses forgiveness specifically. If there is a rupture in a relationship, we need to forgive or ask forgiveness, even if we don't know what we did wrong. If we have hurt someone and they refuse forgiveness, we are to ask three times. If forgiveness is not forthcoming after three attempts, people are counseled to "Be not hateful in thine own eyes." Refusing to forgive a person who asks sincerely is considered as great an offense as the original indiscretion or offense.

As with Buddhism, the greater purpose is to maintain a loving connection: "I don't know what I've done, but if I hurt you in any way, I'm sorry. That was never my intent. I value you as my friend." This reminds us that misunderstandings and deep hurts are part of the human condition. As our consciousness becomes bigger than the problem, and our love more vast than thinking about who did what, we pierce our armored hearts and bring ourselves back into connection with each other.

Some people rush to forgiveness to appear enlightened. This only perpetuates wearing a mask and being alienated from your authentic self. Forgiveness is often a process that involves going through stages of feeling hurt, angry, sad, or harboring thoughts of revenge. We may need to feel the full impact of these emotions before we can step back and feel compassion and understanding. This takes us to the heart of Buddhism, which is to see through all our conditioning and into the human heart, to have mercy and compassion, to be tender toward ourselves and others.

Most often, our real task is to forgive ourselves. If I say negative things about my partner to others, I need to look at how I am harming myself with my actions. How am I tearing apart the threads of my integrity? Why did I break this covenant? Why did I harm this relationship? It's important to see that whatever we do to another, we are doing to ourselves. If we harbor anger, we are the one with the clenched jaw and the armored heart. The separation we make from another makes a separation within us. Thus, self-forgiveness and lovingkindness become our daily practice.

I spoke with my friend Ruth about forgiveness. She is a treasured friend, happily married for thirty-seven years. Her life is centered around service, creativity, and bringing joy to others as she radiates warmth, generosity, and humor.

"Forgiveness is embedded so deeply in our relationship and in our Christian faith," she told me. "You cannot love if you're holding anything against someone. Relationships have to be entwined with forgiveness. It's the core and basis of being able to love. Forgiveness stems from our faith; we forgive because we are forgiven. A lot of people who haven't gotten that insight hate to think they have anything to be forgiven for. But no matter how much we try to be perfect, we are all caught in this inadequacy. When you forgive, you can start to look at people with eyes that can truly love. I see it as a gift from the Holy Spirit and God. I believe that every single person deserves to be loved, no matter what their human inadequacies."

When we can forgive each other, we can reconcile nearly anything. Whether you see forgiveness from a Buddhist or Christian perspective, the essence is the same. We are all fallible, imperfect beings.

Reconciliation is the blessing of two people stepping past hurt, pride, and ego, and revealing their hearts. We go from separation to connection, from dissonance to harmony. We unmask our buried grief and hurt. Sometimes, we weep together. We were out of harmony, separated, and now we come together back into harmony, into the "us" place. The more we reconcile with everyone in our lives through our capacity to forgive, the more we come into oneness with ourselves. Through our daily relations of forgiving and being forgiven, we start to experience the marvelous vastness of loving. That's what makes life so beautiful and allows us to enter into loving relationships with others.

PART SEVEN

MAKE FRIENDS
WITH CONFLICT

38 THE ART OF HANDLING CONFLICT

Just as any great musical composition is a skillful flow from tension to release, from activity to quiet, from intensity to ease, handling differences and problems is an intrinsic part of weaving a relationship. The artfulness of the whole is the sum of these parts skillfully woven together.

Crucial to the artful handling of conflict is the commitment of two people to enter into the "us" circle—to agree to be honest, vulnerable, struggle together, know each other, and work for the good of the relationship while not abandoning their individual needs. The commitment to the relationship provides a safe container for differences, the implication being that we're in this together and we'll work it out. Without safety and trust, conflict carries the risk of loss and hurt. As a result, people tend to try to protect themselves by holding back or trying to control their partner.

Sometimes, we feel torn between our yearning for heartfelt connection and the desire to hide our not-so-pleasant stuff and wear a mask of being cool, or having it all together. But remember, the appearance of composure pales in comparison to loving touch, humor, warmth, and a tender embrace. To have a relationship is to be vulnerable.

To help yourself be willing to address conflict, allow yourself to feel your longing for joy, connection, vitality, and sexual passion. Let yourself know that through your efforts to be more open, you create a pathway to deeper connection. If your relationship is drifting into a fog, don't wait passively, hoping things will get better. Remember, you are a vital part of the equation, and you have the power to make a difference.

39 MEETING OUR DIFFERENCES: FIGHT THE GOOD FIGHT

> *Whenever there is confusion (and turmoil is confu-*
> *sion—it's just a little noisier), you know there is*
> *something that somebody, or two people, do not*
> *want to see. . . . . This does not mean it is worthy of*
> *fear. Enter into it. Here's a great possibility that just*
> *beneath turmoil there is a wonderful oneness that*
> *you are both still frightened of.*
> —*Pat Rodegast,* EMMANUEL'S BOOK II

It's natural that any two people come together with different temperaments, habits, experiences, values, education, knowledge, fears, desires, and conditioning. The question is not whether we will have conflict as a couple, it's how we'll name it and deal with it. The skillful handling of differences creates safety, trust, and in large part determines the depth and success of a relationship. People usually get locked into dead-end patterns because they don't know another way.

We need to distinguish between a conflict of egos and approaching our differences in the spirit of finding the best solution for the individuals *and* the couple. To the extent we are in conflict with ourselves—disowning, rejecting, and ashamed of the parts we have labeled bad—conflict will feel contentious and scary because we are actually resisting self-knowledge. The more we are fully aware and accepting of ourselves, the more relaxed we will be with conflict, because there is no ego to defend and nothing to be ashamed of. We're simply seeking understanding, and a bridge to a solution.

I invite you to think of dealing constructively with conflict as a process that can be learned. It is a worthy process that requires honesty, vulnerability, and a willingness to listen, reflect on oneself, and change. Conflict can open a pathway to richer knowledge of oneself and one's partner and lead to deeper intimacy.

For many, conflict feels threatening. They enter the "conflict ring" with boxing gloves on to defend the "I," "me," and "mine." It carries the risk of fights, hurt feelings, shame, antagonism, winners, losers, and even abandonment. That's why a conflict of egos without a path toward resolution leaves so many people in fear of bringing up differences. The mind goes back and forth between wanting to say something and fearing that it will result in more turmoil and frustration.

Resolving conflict requires a softening of our identification with our ego, which wants to be right and to win. At the same time, it requires having a grounded, yet fluid, sense of self. We need to stop blaming our partner, and explore our part in the conflict. We may need to ask some difficult, and possibly embarrassing, questions: Am I determined to get my way? Am I thinking only of myself? Am I giving in or sacrificing my values because I'm afraid?

The process involves naming the disagreement, employing a process of mediation, finding solutions, and implementing them.

The idea of mediation might conjure up the need for a third person, but what I am talking about here is finding the mediator within yourself. The internal mediator helps us relinquish our attachments to our ideas and beliefs, and reminds us that unity and love are the highest good for both ourselves and our partner. Your internal mediator can listen to both sides of a dispute and enter into dialogue. This opens you both up to the possibility of bridging your differences.

To mediate a conflict means that we enter into the "us" place, where we are concerned with the needs of both individuals *and* the welfare of the relationship. Instead of doing battle to win, mediation helps us move toward listening, understanding, and comprehending what the conflict is all about. This necessitates revealing our needs and feelings. It is crucial to remember that we cannot mediate and at the same time remain distant and intellectual. It is our vulnerability that makes us transparent to each other, softens our anger, opens our hearts to each other, and leads to resolution.

We enter into mediation with the intention of finding a win-win solution. In this arena, we connect through our differences. Thus, conflict becomes a call to listen, reflect, reach deep, understand, see the other person's point of view, and find a workable solution for both people. It also implies a willingness to change.

If we approach mediation from a spiritual perspective, it's about seeking the truth, stepping out of habituated patterns, and living in reality. It's about coming into the present instead of being controlled by old fears. As we reveal ourselves, we become allies on the spiritual journey.

Now let's look at the process of finding solutions to problems. As you read the following definition of "solve," let the meaning of the words sink in. As you will see, they are about gaining a deeper knowledge of a situation, of exploring, knowing, and understanding. Solving is not just looking for an answer to a one-time question. It is a mind-set we carry with us that seeks to unravel, unfold, and illuminate our lives. It's about being open and awake.

Definitions of solve:

1. *To find an answer or solution for a problem or difficulty*
   Synonyms: Fix, resolve, work, work out
   Related: Decide, determine, settle
2. *To find an explanation or solution for something obscure, mysterious, or incomprehensible*
   Synonyms: Break, clear up, decipher, dissolve, figure out, puzzle out, resolve, unfold, unravel
   Related: Enlighten, illuminate, construe, elucidate, explain, interpret

I love the definition of "solve" as finding an explanation or solution for something obscure, mysterious, or incomprehensible. So often, people are stuck in conflict and are mystified as to why it keeps happening, and why it's so hard to stop. The answer lies in recognizing when we're in a child state and projecting authority figures on our partners. We need to drop into a deeper level of self-awareness and relinquish our attachment to the past.

Referring again to the above definition, it suggests that solving a problem leads toward enlightenment and illumination. That's because the capacity for handling conflict directly reflects our ability to experience and accept all our feelings and emotions, so we can be open and real. This allows us to come into present time and deal with what's actually at hand, *and* find solutions in the "us" place.

A true solution feels good (or at least workable) for the couple and both individuals. This doesn't mean two people totally agree on lifestyle, parenting, or spending money, but they find some common ground, and are willing to be responsive to each other over time—to listen to each other's ideas, to consider doing things a different way, to read, learn, or become more aware of their motivations.

While some solutions are more of a one-time decision—to buy a car or take a vacation—most decisions are an ongoing process that reflect our investment in the relationship. It helps to remember that when we have conflict about taking care of household tasks, children, pets, money, saving time for each other, or making love, we are also saying, I want you here with me, I need to know you're invested in this relationship. I want us to be a team.

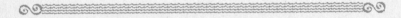

♱Ø PRACTICE CONFLICT PREVENTION

It might seem odd that I'm including a section on conflict prevention after saying that conflict is natural, normal, and an important part of relationships. While processing tensions and difficulties is important, sometimes we mistake for intimacy the endless processing of thoughts and feelings. Every little nuance of our relationship becomes subject to analysis and exploration. We think that talking is the key to feeling close. More likely, it's a way we resist deeper contact with ourselves.

We solve conflict so we can feel clear and remove any blocks between us.

Conflict prevention comes from pleasure, commitment, perceptiveness, forgiveness, owning up to one's feelings, playfulness, and making love throughout the day by listening, touching, being helpful, and giving each other our full attention. When there is a flow of lovingkindness, thank-yous come easily, agreements are kept with great care, and there is a balance of give-and-take. No one is left wondering if he or she is loved. When we feel a full, rich love between us, we are naturally more forgiving of each other.

When people feel loved and appreciated, mistakes or oversights on the part of a partner are seen as exceptions and rarely taken personally. For example, if one person forgets to pick something up at the store or is grumpy, the partner shrugs it off: "He's forgetful" or "She's just under stress." I spoke with Ruth, who has had a deeply loving relationship for thirty-seven years. She said, "There hasn't been a lot of conflict because we're perceptive, we apologize for our mistakes, we help each other see the big picture, and we enjoy being together. Our relationship is rooted in our Christian faith and forgiveness is central to that faith. It's such a huge part, because it means we can let go of anger or judgments and come back to the love. We have so much acceptance for each other."

A major form of conflict prevention is simply having fun together and sharing experiences. Like a spring rain awakening a garden, shared joy, quiet time, playfulness, awaken us to each other. The more we feel love and happiness in a relationship, the less important our differences feel.

Another aspect of conflict prevention is to take care of those prickly little moments when some comment or remark leads to tension. Unresolved or unspoken feelings and hurts often create a vague dullness or a sterile distance, often punctuated with sly digs, withdrawal, and an occasional outburst of anger. If you feel yourself even sliding in this direction, catch yourself, push through whatever fear you have, and bring up these minor irritations.

Don't let the little things mount up. If I feel hurt that my partner didn't seem responsive or caring last Tuesday when I hurt my knee, and I don't say anything, it will be a little wiggle in my mind next Friday when she's a few minutes late. Then, on Sunday, when she doesn't help with the dishes after breakfast, I will feel even more irritation building. If I can truly let go of these things, then I need not say anything. However, if the memories waft through my mind when we're making love and my body starts to withdraw, I know I need to explore my feelings and say something. If, after I had hurt my knee, I had said, "I really felt you were distant when we went to the emergency room. What was going on with you?" and we talk and I really listen to her until the air clears, then any new event will be a small deal, not burdened with the buildup of other, earlier situations.

The agreement to keeping a relationship clear is one of the most profound commitments we can make. It implies a commitment to know ourselves, to sort out our internal censors from our voice of wisdom, and often to speak up, even when we are afraid. It means letting go of the outcome and taking the risk of feeling wrong, silly, or vulnerable.

Remember, if you feel uncomfortable and start withdrawing or building up resentments, it's your responsibility to bring yourself back into the relationship and open up the dialogue. When you blame your partner, or hide your feelings, you have stepped out of the "us" place.

Probably the most damaging thing we can do in a relationship is to withdraw emotionally and stockpile hurts and anger. Holding back leads to a buildup in pressure that may eventually lead to an explosion. Someone wakes up one day and says, "What happened to our love? Where did the joy go? Where is the sexual desire? I want out!" The partner is dumbfounded: "I had no idea." It's so important to notice tensions and take them seriously when you feel the vitality slipping out of your relationship.

Easing daily tensions can be very simple when people have self-awareness and can reveal their inner experience—including their child states.

Our mutual self-revelations soften our irritation and bring us back to love and understanding. When we both reach deep, own our part, and clear the air, there is nothing left to block the love that naturally flows between us.

41 RECOGNIZE COUNTERFEIT CONFLICTS

While life will always hand us problems to solve, there are what I call "counterfeit conflicts" that don't have much to do with what's really going on in present time. Throughout the dance of relationship, it's important to sort out ego-based reactions from childhood that need our individual attention, as opposed to true conflicts in the present that need us to negotiate our differences.

In troubled couples, people often start fights or create dramas in order to avoid their fear and emptiness. This is extremely common when there are active addictions or dependency in the relationship. We fight over red-herring issues and focus on our partner instead of focusing on ourselves. A man says he can't be sexually attracted unless his partner loses weight, but doesn't realize he plays a part in his own sexual arousal.

Another cause of counterfeit conflict is when people, having adopted the belief that the world is hostile, are hyperalert to any possibility of rejection or insensitivity, and repeatedly pounce on their partner with claims that he or she is mean, uncaring, and so on. We need to ask ourselves repeatedly, "What was really said? How did I filter it through my own internal belief system?" Of course, this implies that we recognize that we have an internal belief system about the world that colors our perceptions about people's intentions.

Counterfeit conflicts stem from hardwired nervous system responses to previous experiences. When we yell at our partner for being late, it might be a displaced scream at a mother who was unreliable. We panic when our partner withdraws and rush in to "find out what's wrong" or "get her to talk." When I've helped people track the source of these eruptions of emotions, we inevitably find the roots in childhood losses, trauma, or neglect that resulted in beliefs of being unlovable, unseen, powerless, or inadequate.

For example, Mary felt panic whenever her partner withdrew. We traced it back to a time when, as a little girl, she found her mother lying on the couch, passed out from drinking. Mary thought she was dead. As we cleared this old trauma, she no longer had a panic reaction when her lover withdrew. She didn't like it, but she could express her feelings as an adult, saying, "I don't like it when you blank out and refuse to talk." She could then go about her day without obsessing about it.

Couples who find themselves in repetitive fights that reflect childlike states—"Don't tell me what to do," "Don't leave me"— often need individual psychotherapy to clear the source of these automatic reactions. Rumi writes, "Show me the way to the ocean, break these small containers." With that sentiment in mind, here are some steps to help us break free of the small containers that keep us stuck in repetitive counterfeit arguments. (Ground rule: Keep the focus on yourself and do not blame your partner.)

1. Notice repetitive arguments and acknowledge them to each other. Agree you want to do something different.

2. Ask yourself, "How old do I feel in this argument? Very young? Adolescent?" Tell your partner about this.

3. Ask yourself, "What are we really arguing about?" Explore this with your partner. Usually, there's an undercurrent of not feeling loved, valued, noticed, or respected that needs to be addressed.

4. Tune in to your feelings and peel them back to see if there's another one underneath. Keep peeling back until you reach a place that feels very real to you. This may take practice. Tell your partner about your experience with this. When a person can say, "I feel lonely when you spend so much time away" rather than "You are so insensitive to my needs," we take the conversation to a quieter, deeper level of vulnerability. It is from this place that people usually can hear each other.

5. Become aware of what you are truly wanting and needing from your partner, and let him or her know.

6. Talk about whatever you are willing to do in response to your partner's request. Make a concrete plan; don't use vague language such as: "I'll help you around the house" or "I'll respect you more." Spell it out. "I'll vacuum Monday night when you're out." "I'll shop and cook on Saturday." "I promise to stop calling you lazy or clumsy when I'm frustrated."

7. Voice your appreciation for your partner. Again, be specific.

Following these steps may help you crack your shell and feel more expansive in your relationship. Other possible avenues of help are to talk with a friend, be in a support group, read books on relationships or spirituality, or seek counseling. You can also talk with friends. Just having contact with a wide range of people increases the odds that someone will say something helpful about your situation or open your mind to a new perspective.

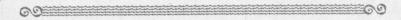

42 REMEMBER, WE ARE ANIMALS WITH A NEOCORTEX: RECOGNIZE FIGHT, FLIGHT, AND FREEZE REACTIONS

Recently, someone commented on a radio show that the most dreaded phrase for a man to hear from a woman is: "Honey, we need to talk." If clearing conflict is so essential to keeping relationships alive and vital, why do so many couples collude in avoiding it? One reason is that we haven't learned the basics for respectful conflict solution.

A second reason is that for many, the prospect of conflict sends their pulse racing, their adrenaline pumping, their stomach churning. Why is this? They are experiencing a hardwired basic survival reaction that was probably set in place as a child and reinforced over the years. They have literally fallen out of the neocortex. In psychological terms, it's called "flooding." In popular jargon, we might say that we're freaking out or going numb with fear. It usually has almost nothing to do with the current situation.

To understand survival responses, consider the functions of the three parts of the brain. According to Dr. Paul MacLean, a brain researcher, we are essentially animals with a neocortex—the frontal part of the brain capable of reason, insight, reflection, anticipation, and humanitarian behavior. Our brain stem, often called the reptilian brain, is involved in self-preservation—

hunting, homing, mating, establishing territory, and fighting. The midbrain or limbic system, which we also share with other animals, deals with the emotional feelings that guide behavior. It is the source of those "knee-jerk" reactions that seem to go off on their own. Here's why.

As a child, whenever we felt our safety threatened, we were likely to go into a hyper-state of arousal—fast pulse, sweating, adrenaline pumping—and seek ways to alleviate our fear, terror, and anxiety. In this heightened state, our brain was able to register, in vivid detail, colors, sounds, smells, and other details associated with the trauma of the moment, along with our emotional state. All of this got hardwired into the nervous system.

Here's the crucial factor: because the limbic system is capable of generalizing and does not distinguish between current and past time, anything that reminds us of that early situation can recreate that same intense reaction.

For example, Jim was often criticized or called stupid by his mother and his first wife of twenty-five years. When he married his true love—his former college sweetheart—an innocent question of hers, such as "Do you know where the keys are?" would get a sudden retort: "You just think I'm stupid." From years of criticism, he had generalized to believe that any question he couldn't immediately answer meant he was stupid, and that everything was automatically his fault. His response, "You just think I'm stupid," signified that he was operating out of the limbic system. We need to raise our awareness of these automatic responses if we are to have a relationship in present time. Otherwise, we are prisoners of the past and projecting our psychological history onto our partner.

Here are some typical cues to fight, flight, and freeze reactions to remember when you have conflict with someone:

Fight responses: blame, counterattack, accuse, make up excuses, analyze, criticize, get defensive, change the subject, discount what the other person is saying, start crying, become intellectual, talk in generalities, get the other person to feel sorry for you, get the other person to feel guilty, tell jokes, get violent.

Flight responses: leave the scene, run away, walk out the door.

Freeze responses: go blank, go numb, lose your voice, disassociate.

The first step is to realize we're sliding into one of these states, and if we're not too overwhelmed, we can say to our partner, "I'm afraid right now I'm having an old reaction, and I need to calm down before I can deal with this." We can ask ourselves, "What was really said? Is there really danger?" We can remind ourselves, "That was then, this is now."

In such a state, do not try to proceed with the discussion. When we're flooded, it's virtually impossible to function with reason, because we're in a state of hyperarousal and living in the past. Your quarrel will have virtually nothing to do with the present. These responses can be fairly mild or intense. I remember when, as a client in a supervision group, I became so afraid, I felt completely disconnected from my body. The supervisor kept pressing me to talk, so I just made up whatever I thought she wanted to hear to get her to back off. Everything seemed like a blur. I just wanted her to leave me alone. Another woman in the group asked me a question and the supervisor said that my answer was crummy and I had no idea why. I felt horrible, yet powerless to do anything, to say anything. When we are in a fear state, we are basically in survival mode, disconnected from our neocortex, and unable to draw on our inner resources.

This doesn't mean we need to disengage completely. We can sit together, and if possible lighten up about the whole thing. One time in a couple therapy session, when a woman started snapping and getting insistent, she suddenly stopped herself, and said to her partner, "Oh God, there I go, catch me." A smile emerged on her partner's face, which had previously looked tense. "How can I catch you?" he said.

"Just touch me," she answered. When he leaned over and put his hand on her arm, she started to cry and visibly relax. A few minutes later, she remarked, "That was what I needed." As a result of that interchange, they agreed that when she clicked into that demanding, angry state, she could just say, "Catch me," and he would touch her, or if she didn't catch herself, he would lean over and touch her. Thus they became allies in breaking the predictable negative cycle that usually followed her demanding, angry outbursts. The point is to find a way to intervene as a couple on how you handle survival responses.

There are many ways couples can become allies to handle these survival responses. I often ask one member of a couple, "What would you like your partner to say or do when she or he sees you slide into that behavior?" People have come up with statements or questions such as, "Are you feeling stressed? Do you need a break?" Some people want to be touched. The key is to retrain the nervous system by getting into an "us" place when there is distress, instead of acting like a frightened animal.

Instead of withdrawing or feeling ashamed, it becomes something the couple handles together. That way, if one person says, "I need to calm down for twenty minutes," the partner understands and is supportive instead of hurling accusations: "You always run away, you never talk to me!" or some other misinterpretation. The more a couple becomes allies, the more they create a secure "us" place. This opens the possibility of coming up with creative solutions to deal with these old flight, fight, and freeze responses.

As a last thought, we can also have positive memories wired into the nervous system. The smell of our mother's face powder, an old song we danced to in high school, or a poem our father read at Christmas can send a ripple of warm feelings through the body as they rekindle happy memories from the past. We can build these positive memories into our relationships by shared pleasure, kindness, and joy.

43 RECOGNIZE THE MANY FACES OF ANGER

The same wind that uproots trees
makes the grasses shine

And the motion of the body comes from
the spirit like a waterwheel
that's held in a stream

The inhaling-exhaling is from spirit,
now angry, now peaceful.
                    —*Rumi, "The Grasses"*

It is crucial to understand the many faces of anger so that we can be both authentic and respectful in our relationships. There are many aspects of anger on the spiritual path that are relevant to relationships and internal awareness. Exploring anger is a crucial aspect of self-knowledge and the entryway to experiencing love.

We can approach anger in the following ways:

1. Anger as a natural survival response
2. Anger that becomes automatic
3. Anger as a frustrated desire or need—an attachment
4. The danger of repressed anger
5. Sorting out the difference between anger and rage
6. Using anger constructively in relationships—expressing our needs

We all feel anger. Much of the spiritual literature, including some Buddhist writings, refers to anger as a negative emotion to be controlled and eradicated. It's poison medicine. I have been at Buddhist talks where anger was listed as one of the "bad" emotions we should get rid of. Some people say you are part of the cause of war even if you have just a tiny bit of anger in you. I disagree.

If everything is made of one energy, then anger, sadness, happiness are all a form of that energy. I agree fully with Pema Chodron's teachings that we want to make friends with every aspect of our feelings and thoughts because they are all Buddha energy. We make no separation.

Ultimately, I agree that most of the time anger is a cover for other feelings, and is often misplaced and unproductive. Yet, we need to make friends with it and thoroughly understand it so we transform it rather than deny it.

Anger has many sources and forms of expression. It can be just as harmful to deny anger and have it create havoc in our bodies, as to repeatedly explode with it. Indeed, hiding anger, repressing it, or calling it shameful is what often sets off the rage explosions that are so damaging to relationships.

Being aware of our anger and exploring its source can be a powerful means for awakening. Some of the strongest cultural messages surrounding anger become entrenched in our belief system and we start to think they are real. An angry woman is often seen as unfeminine, a bitch, a man-hater, and a radical, to name a few.

Men, by being taught to deny their fear, sadness, and vulnerability, often channel these feelings into anger, which becomes a cover for more authentic feelings. Others deny their anger and live in a rigid body. You and your partner might want to take some time to talk about all the messages you received about anger. What has it meant in your life and what do you do with it? Get scared, have a headache, eat, hide, want sex, feign a smile, tell yourself you're bad, or explode?

Reading through the different aspects of anger might provide more ideas for your conversation.

Anger as a Natural Survival Response

One form of anger is a normal, biological, survival response to emergencies or danger—being hurt, invaded, or encroached upon. A hot flash spikes through us, and we secrete adrenaline, which gives us energy to act. Animals bare their teeth, hiss, or strike out when threatened. As adults, survival anger can help us protect ourselves and set limits when being exploited or attacked. We need to be able to respond with a firm "Stop," "No," "That's not all right with me," without feeling we're committing a crime.

Unfortunately, many people feel unsafe in the world because this survival mechanism that senses danger—a kind of internal alarm system—had been conditioned out of them by rigid, controlling parents and social norms. Instead of moving toward action when they are threatened, they freeze and feel paralyzed to protect themselves. If we're becoming sentimental about someone who has abused us, our anger helps us recall the violation and helps us remember to take care of ourselves and not subject ourselves to further injury. And remember, being able to say no and set limits is a prerequisite for feeling safe enough to say a wholehearted yes.

Going a step deeper, we need to remember that fear is often the initial feeling that precedes anger.

It looks like this:

Event $\Longrightarrow$ fear $\Longrightarrow$ feel unable to act $\Longrightarrow$ unmet needs

$\Longrightarrow$ frustrations/anger

Anger That Becomes Automatic

The counterpart of having useful survival anger that helps us set limits is when it goes on automatic and is not related to the current situation. One defense we develop in response to childhood trauma is an automatic anger that gives us a sense of control—if I can't be loved, at least I can keep people away by intimidating them. This extends to adulthood, when we repeatedly misread situations as dangerous or threatening and, as a result, we project a hostile front. It is extremely important to recognize these automatic anger responses, because they keep us locked in the past, are damaging to relationships, and produce the chronic secretion of stress hormones. This keeps us perpetually agitated and can lead to depression.

The axiom "Have your feelings" or "Share your feelings" doesn't apply to automatic anger. It's not fair to discharge this kind of anger on the people around you because it has nothing to do with the current situation. We need to pull back, breathe, and remember, these are nervous system reflexes based on old perceptions. Changing this response will take effort, because automatic anger was often the only way we knew how to feel safe in a world that appeared so unloving and hostile. We start by thanking that angry part of ourself for working so hard to protect us. Then we can say a gentle *That was then, this is now* and proceed from there.

Anger as a Frustrated Desire or Attachment

This is the aspect of anger that applies to most of us most of the time. Usually, when we are angry, we have an attachment to someone or something being different than it is. If we go beneath our anger and recognize our attachments, we can gain tremendous self-awareness. I've learned to recognize a place in me that feels like a very hurt three-year-old that gets insistent on being understood. It triggers a particular physical feeling and quality right in my solar plexus. When I feel it, I simply take a breath, observe it, and don't act—at least on a good day.

If we get in the habit of noticing our attachments—wanting things to be different than they are—we can go beneath our anger reaction and recognize our wants. When you feel anger rising, take a breath, slow down, and ask yourself, what am I wanting or needing? This will help your inner experience shift dramatically so you aren't transmitting anger energy all around you and scaring other people away. From this place, you can make respectful requests. Instead of being accusatory—"You never hug me when you come home"—you can say, "Hey, beautiful, how about a hug?" It seems like such a small switch, but it takes us from an angry kid stance to being a grown-up making a forthright request. From this place of vulnerability, we are much more likely to connect with others and bring the conversation into the "us" place.

I want to end by saying how important our intent is: we can say, I have an *intention* to notice my attachments, I have the *intention* of not always reacting so fast. I have the *intention* of being more aware. It sends a message throughout our body that opens the way for change. It's not a demand placed on ourselves—which is a form of attachment—it's like gently opening a door to see what's on the other side.

Notice the Danger of Repressed Anger

As I mentioned earlier, stockpiling anger is one of the most harmful things we can do to ourselves and others. If we're trying not to be angry, but we know we are, it lives inside us and transmits a powerful signal to others.

Repressed anger is when we so thoroughly disown our anger that we're convinced we don't have any. However, if we listen to our thoughts and attune to the physical sensations in our bodies, we can start to unearth it. Here are some ways to tap into your disowned anger:

1. Your self-image is that you're mellow, sweet, or kind—a "good guy," a "loving woman." You often say, "I'm not angry. I'm not upset."
2. You speak in a flat, pale, quiet voice with little affect or power. It might have a whiny or pleading quality to it. You make indirect hints or remarks that make you feel queasy inside and often lead to tension in the relationship.
3. You feel a twinge of delight when someone meets with hardship—they lose a job, gain weight, get divorced, or have other problems.
4. You frequently judge others and are quick to notice their shortcomings. You bond with friends by criticizing others. You subtly set people against each other by revealing confidences or making indirect remarks.
5. You periodically have numerous physical symptoms: headaches, stomachaches, muscle tension, tight jaw, and so on.

6. You are often anxious, get depressed, or stay superbusy (an agitated depression). When you slow down the pace, you feel sad, empty, or lack energy.
7. Your partner has volatile anger.
8. You put off doing what you say you'll do. You make agreements and don't follow through.
9. You withdraw, are sullen, pout, get afraid to talk, or blank out in a conflict situation.
10. You have a feeling of separation from people as if there is a veil between you. You withhold affection, sex, kindness, or warmth.
11. You complain but don't ask for what you want.
12. You can lose your temper and blow up, but it's difficult to ask for what you want, set limits, or stand up for yourself.

Remember, the purpose of tapping into your anger is to make friends with it. Otherwise it's like an enemy within, draining your energy and keeping you afraid. Many of us started repressing anger for a very good reason a long time ago—perhaps we were punished, shamed, ignored, or threatened with abandonment if we said no or got angry at our caregivers. But we're not children anymore, and we can dare to open the closet door and shine the light on this frightened, fragmented part of us that needs our mercy, understanding, and compassion. Again, we can remember that everything is Buddha energy. Even that terrified part of us is simply Buddha being afraid.

The Importance of Sorting Out Anger from Rage

Healthy anger is direct, relates to the current situation, and is not attacking or out of control. Rage, on the other hand, comes from taking accumulated hurts that have been stockpiled from the past and exploding with accusations, blame, and hostility. Rage is often a cover-up for shame. Someone has touched a part of us that we've called bad or defective, and to avoid the pain of feeling our shame, we focus outward, often blaming and putting down others.

Some people use rage like an addiction. Just as binge drinkers build up their frustrations during the week and get drunk on Friday night to let off steam, people who constantly rage often do the same. They are disconnected from their feelings, disregard their needs, and fail to ask for what they need or want. Over time, pressure builds, and eventually they aim and fire their fury at whoever happens to be nearby. It's essentially a childlike temper tantrum.

While the outburst may momentarily ease internal stress, the pattern is cyclical and never gets to the heart of the problem. It's also frightening to others. When people are repeatedly the target of rage attacks, or live under the threat of one, they tend to build a shell around their heart as protection. They are on guard, uneasy.

If rage is a problem for you, one key is to recognize the experience of shame. You can start by looking at whatever needs, sorrows, frustrations, and losses you have disowned, rejected, or denied within yourself. Consider what is missing for you in your current situation. What do you need to discuss with your partner? Are you deeply unhappy about something? Commit to dealing with your feelings in a more skillful way. Focus on them, feel them, listen to what you are telling yourself. What is so scared and defended inside? Ask your partner and children to tell you how your rage attacks affect them. And truly listen.

Using Anger Constructively in Relationships— Expressing Our Needs

There is no rest for a messenger 'til the message is delivered.
—Joseph Conrad, THE RESCUE

While rage is toxic to relationships, there are times when we feel angry and need to voice it so it doesn't turn to poison inside, come out in coded messages, or make us anxious, tense, or sick. Many couples have a covert agreement: *I won't get angry at you if you don't get angry at me. We'll be nice.* We identify with an image of how we want to appear rather than being true. This permeates a relationship with fear because there is chronic holding back that reinforces the false belief that anger is dangerous. As a result, the relationship becomes emotionally dulled.

The agreement that helps relationships stay alive is, *"I will say what's bothering me and I will listen to what's bothering you."* This doesn't mean yelling and screaming; it means respectfully saying what's troubling us. As one woman said, "We have agreed to keep clear with each other. If anything is simmering inside, we say it. It could be something such as, 'That hurt my feelings. I don't like it when you use that tone of voice with me.' We don't always say it right away; sometimes it's better to wait until we've cooled off or find a time when we're both able to be attentive. The more we do it, the easier it gets. It's made a great difference in our relationship—it's so important to deal with irritation and anger, or whatever keeps us apart."

We can use the basic assertiveness formula, I feel/felt angry when you said/did _____. This helps people understand the effect of their behavior. If there is trust in the relationship, both partners will want to hear when their mate is upset because they want to know the truth. And they will want to do something about it. Anger or hurt will not be taken lightly or ignored because both partners are committed to loving each other well. This willing attention to the feelings and needs of the partner keeps a relationship from sliding into constant complaining, nagging, or unhappiness.

We need to remember that nearly always there is a request underlying our anger. Unfortunately, many people find it easier to chronically complain rather than be direct with their anger and ask for their underlying needs to be met. Why is this?

Voicing our needs opens the possibility of a richer, more satisfying relationship, yet it also carries the risk of finding out our needs will not be met. To the ego, this is frightening because a refusal feels like a withdrawal of love. From a spiritual perspective, however, it is just the *what is* of the moment—people say yes, people say no, and it's up to us to accept it. Very often, if there is a no we can find other ways to meet our needs and desires. If we remember that living by the truth is the best we can do, then our highest wish is for both of us to be honest.

Some people say they don't get angry, but they are repeatedly showing it with their demands. Here's how to recognize the difference between a request and a demand. If our partner says no to a request, and we pout, feel resentful, or try to convince him or her to give in, we know it was really a demand. We need to feel the anger in our response and look at how we're creating our suffering with our attachments.

We become at one with ourselves when we are at ease with every part of ourselves. When we explore the complex interweaving of fear, anger, and needs and learn to be direct and open, we will feel a profound shift in our relationships. It will allow the river of spirit to flow more freely through us, connecting us to each other and to the universal love that lives at the center of our being.

Explore Your Style of Handling Conflict

According to John Gottman, who researched relationships for twenty years, styles of handling conflict vary but generally fall into three categories: avoidant, validating, and volatile. Each style works for different people and each has its downside. For example, Gottman found that volatile couples, while being the most passionate and close, sometimes run the risk of crossing the line into sarcasm and hurtful remarks. The avoidant style, while more calm and polite, sometimes runs the risk of leaving the relationship flat or dull because the partners are less spontaneous and too much gets swept under the rug. The validating couples, meanwhile, listen very carefully and are good at negotiating, compromising, and being good-natured. But the downside is that they often sacrifice their passion and personal development in order to maintain closeness in the relationship. *The important point was that all the successful couples perceived that they could talk about anything and it would be resolved.*

As a couple, the style we adopt will reflect our temperaments and personalities. If two people come together with different styles, it's useful to talk about them: "I flare up momentarily, then it's over." "I like to take time to listen. Yelling scares me." "I need time to think things over before answering." This dialogue may be ongoing. You might want to talk about any changes you would like to make as a couple. For example, one woman told me, "We use more of an avoidant style, but I'd like to be freer to just speak up and not be so careful." Another said, "I'm ready to calm down a bit. I think we are too volatile and some days I'd like to be quieter, or just let things go."

The traits that block resolution to conflict and are generally harmful to relationships are what Gottman calls the four horsemen of the apocalypse—criticism, defensiveness, contempt, and stonewalling. If you learn to recognize these automatic responses, you will take a big step toward a more peaceful, pleasurable relationship. It takes courage and faith to explore these traits in ourselves. It may help to bring your focus to all you have to gain by dropping these ego-based ways of relating. They are old habits born of fear. They may have served you well a long time ago, but in giving birth to a language of love, we need to see our beloved, not as a feared ghost from the past, but as this dear person we have taken as our special one.

44   WHAT TO DO WHEN YOU REACH AN IMPASSE

Sometimes, couples find themselves deadlocked when it comes to money, values, spending time, or interests. The difference between successful couples and troubled couples rests in how the individuals interpret and react to the situation.

As an example, Charles and Elizabeth have a strong, long-lasting, vital relationship. However, Charles finds tremendous pleasure in training dogs for his frequent hunting trips. Liz dislikes hunting and is extremely devoted to donating time, money, and energy to organizations serving people in need. The conflict hits a collision point when a choice arises between donating money for a homeless shelter versus buying an expensive new hunting dog.

"I have to have patience and understand that helping others is extremely important to her," Charles said when I spoke with them. "But it takes a lot of acceptance because she's gone a lot and I wish she were here more."

I asked Charles about buying hunting dogs.

"Well, as a matter of fact, I am just about to buy another one," he said.

"How do you handle it as a couple?" I asked.

He paused. "I tell her I'm going to buy it, and I explain that it's important to me and I hope she can understand." He paused and said with a smile, "She accepts it, but I can't say I win her over. It causes stress and strain, and we don't talk about it much. But we both know that's the way it is and that we're not going to change each other."

"Would you say you have a truce about it?"

Charles laughed. "Yes! That's about what it is." He immediately shifted gears, speaking in a brighter tone. "But it's just a small part of our relationship. We have so much going for us. We've been married forty-six years, and we're not going to let some little thing tear us apart. We share a lot and have rather different lives. I think it works well. If we shared all our interests and time, it would get boring."

When I spoke with Elizabeth, she was amused at Charles's perception that she was away a lot. "I could say the same thing about all the time he spends hunting," she said. "Aren't we funny how we see things from our perspective?"

In talking about spending money on a hunting dog, she referred back to a time many years earlier: "He went out and bought this extremely expensive dog. I was very upset. All I could think of was: 'How could anyone spend so much money on a dog when there are so many people going hungry? That's it. This is just too much.' I thought about leaving and cried myself to sleep. But that night I started to think about holidays, and how I'd miss him, and I realized it was not important enough to get a divorce over. . . .

It seems kind of funny now, looking back." She agreed with Charles's comment that they definitely have differences but don't dwell on them. She added, "Once the decision is made, we drop it. We don't bring it up again."

Elizabeth and Charles handled their differences like relationship pros. Their behavior demonstrates all the necessary elements of managing differing values. Here's what was so effective about how they handled their conflict:

1. They both acknowledged their differences and expressed their feelings and wants openly; Elizabeth talked about how upset she had been, and allowed herself to cry over spending money on the hunting dogs.

2. They both accepted each other's right to their passions even though they couldn't relate to them. This affirmed the "us" place *and* the individual rights of each of them.

3. They maintained their separate identities. Neither one sacrificed a deeply held value or interest to placate the other. Charles bought the hunting dog. Elizabeth gave as much money as possible to social justice organizations.

4. Neither one placated the other by changing their behavior. Elizabeth didn't start hunting with Charles to be a "good wife." Charles did not increase the time he gave to peace and justice activities, although he already gave substantially.

5. They did not add layers of interpretation to the other's behavior—as in, "You don't respect me when you do that," "If you loved me, you'd . . ." It was just seen as a difference.

6. Once the decision was made, they let it go and did not dwell on it.

7. They shifted their focus to all the ways they enjoyed and appreciated each other.

From the start of a relationship, couples are challenged to move through a process of accepting each other's differences. Let's look at Jessie and David. Early in their marriage, Jessie wanted David to attend Jewish holiday services with her and their two children. He staunchly refused.

"I'd carry on and try to convince him it was good for the family, and best for all of us," Jessie said. "I took it to mean he didn't care about me and the kids. Then one day I talked to a woman friend who came alone for a gathering and when I asked her if her husband ever came, she said, 'Oh, no, it's not his thing.' She said it so casually, I had this flash of realization: David just doesn't want to come. Same as the way I don't want to go fishing. It doesn't mean anything but that. So I stopped pressuring him to join us, and while I felt sad for a while, it lowered the conflict between us. As I stopped dwelling so much on this one difference, I could more clearly see all the good things in our relationship and the other ways he does show his love."

Differences exist in healthy couples, and sometimes they will sit there like a rock. The point is to set the rock on a shelf and look at it, rather than throwing it at your partner. You don't have to like the rock and you don't have to get rid of it, you simply need to respect that it exists. The task is to make your love bigger than those rocks, so you can experience all of the joys of your relationship.

45 LEARN FAIR-FIGHT RULES

A night full of talking that hurts,
my worst held-back secrets. Everything
has to do with loving and not loving.
This night will pass. . . .
—*Rumi,* THE ESSENTIAL RUMI

To have a "fair fight," we need to agree on ground rules and a clear format for addressing conflict. This creates safety and is a substitute for having an external mediator or third person helping out. If you both have a copy of the ground rules, you can gently remind each other when you get off course. In my couples' workshop, each couple would have another couple sit close by, gently reminding them when they broke the fair-fight guidelines. If you do have another couple interested in learning better ways to handle conflict, you could practice this together. You would learn a lot about each other, realize how "normal" you are, and probably have a few good laughs. Here are some of the basic fair-fight ground rules:

1. Stick to one topic at a time. It's not fair to change the subject, bring up other problems, or refer to past indiscretions or other failings of the partner.
2. Talk in "I" statements: "I'm having a hard time when you . . . ," "I'm frustrated when . . . ," "I would like to . . ." Don't say, "I think it would be best if 'we' . . ." It's important that you each speak for yourself.

3. Avoid statements such as: "You always," "You never," "You did it, too."

4. Go beneath your anger, frustration, or fear to voice your needs, feelings, and wants. You might explain your thinking process so your partner understands how you reached your conclusion.

5. Speak simply in two or three sentences at a time. You don't need to justify or defend yourself.

6. If you get frustrated, breathe deeply and ask for a moment of quiet. If you feel hysterical, petulant, intense, critical, or defensive, call for a time-out. Sit together in silence and calm down before continuing the dialogue.

7. If you get stuck in an argument, take a longer break so each of you can list all of the attachments or demands that you are bringing to the table. Read your list of attachments or demands to each other. "I'm feeling upset because I'm attached to you agreeing with me." "I'm raising my voice and repeating myself because I'm attached to you not interrupting me."

8. Apologize if you cross the line of respect and attack your partner in any way.

9. Remember, the point of conflict is not to be right or to discredit the other. It's to get to the other side so you can enjoy being together.

10. Keep the conflict in the "us" place. It must be focused on finding a win-win solution that both of you can live with.

11. Do your best to keep an open mind to new ways of thinking and handling the situation. It is only your ego that stops you from trying new ways that take you beyond the old conditioned thoughts in your head.

Here is a model of the consensus process used by the Society of Friends for resolving conflict. Having taken part in the process for over twenty years, it lives in me as a guide for maintaining unity while respecting each person's individuality. It is not the only way to approach a conflict, but it is one that has a strong history and has worked for many people. As with everything, take what fits for you, experiment, change it, and, above all, do whatever helps you work things out.

1. Take a moment to sit facing each other, take some deep breaths, relax, and be silent for a few minutes until you feel attuned to each other.

2. Name the conflict. It's like having a chapter title, such as "Money." Then go to the subheadings: "What do we take in?" "What are our expenses?" Then get to the specifics. "How do we pay the heating bill and still have money for me to take a class?" (Note: You *must* agree on the topic for discussion before going forward.)

3. Sit in silence reflecting on the conflict or problem.

4. Have one person say everything he or she has to say about the situation—how they feel, what they want, their thoughts, ideas, hopes, and so on. The other person listens. (Sometimes, it helps to have a talking stick, so the one holding it is the only one allowed to talk.) After a few sentences, the partner can say back what he or she heard. Then reverse the process, with the other person speaking. Continue going back and forth and see if you can build on each other's ideas and feelings. Look for what's possible.

5. Review what you've both said and note any points of agreement.

6. If you need to talk some more, continue. If you start arguing, use a talking stick and repeat what the other person said. This requires us to listen.

7. Brainstorm solutions—put out any ideas, no matter how unusual, weird, impractical, and so on. Let your mind be playful.

8. Have each person state what she or he now sees as a solution. Discuss this together.

9. Agree on a plan, or a partial plan. You may need to gather information before you reach a final solution.

10. Discuss how to implement the plan and who will do what.

11. Stick to the plan. This is your way of saying, I treasure this relationship.

Note: If you don't reach consensus, name the problem, agree to let it season for a while, and set a time to discuss it again.

Finally, remember that solving conflict is a form of intimacy if we listen, respond, and allow our creativity to join in the process. Usually, people feel very close after clearing the air between them or solving a problem.

46 LEARN TO SELF-SOOTHE

Early in life, we get a blueprint for self-soothing. In a loving family, our caregivers delight in being with us. When we reach out, they pick us up and hold us. They coo, smile, and look in our eyes with love. They feed us, sing to us, rock us, give us toys or a cuddly blanket. After a while, we start learning to comfort ourselves. We learn to take comfort in snuggling up to a soft stuffed animal, sucking our thumb, or holding a favorite blanket to our face.

Unfortunately, if life was traumatic, and we were not well loved and comforted, we might have started looking to food, fantasies, possessions, and substances for self-soothing as we got older. Unfortunately, these are counterfeit forms of self-comfort because they stimulate us.

Healthy self-soothing calms the nervous system, stills our mind, and helps us see a broad perspective. This is crucial in relationships, because it empowers us to quiet an angry, racing mind so we don't pick fights or impetuously attack our partner. In the midst of strife, we can take a break to calm ourselves, instead of blurting out words that we'll regret, reaching for chocolate, or taking a drink.

When I ask people how they calm themselves down, they usually mention things like exercise, watching TV, taking a bath, talking with a friend, and so on. This is useful for daily self-soothing and instilling peace of mind in general, but we need to go further, because you can't take a bath in the middle of an argument. At the deepest level, self-soothing is about staying steady in the midst of stress. It's about having an internal reservoir of lovingkindness so we don't tighten up or feel a need to win at all costs. It's about taking a broad view and remembering that this is a momentary happening, not a do-or-die event.

I have listed some self-soothing techniques to help you calm your mind and derail escalating arguments that are going nowhere. Some of these techniques can be used in a heated moment, others are for daily self-soothing. The more you practice them when there is *not* high stress, the more you will be able to engage in momentary self-soothing practices, even in the midst of conflict or frustration.

What You Can Do During an Escalating Conflict

1. Breathe deeply and soften your belly. Notice your breath as it rises and falls. Let your shoulders relax. Let go of any holding inside. Do it again.

2. Repeatedly tell yourself, "It matters, but it's not serious." Have your momentary feelings of being upset, then put the situation in perspective and remember it's not terribly serious. The newspaper doesn't come, our partner snaps at us, our car doesn't start, we don't have the right change for the subway, we're out of eggs when we looked forward to making an omelette. *"It matters, but it's not serious."* This is just a moment in time. It's not a life-or-death situation. It's just *what is*.

3. Ask your partner if she has a request. Take a breath in the midst of an argument and ask, "Do you have a request for me?" Or, if appropriate, "What would you have wanted me to do or say?" This often quiets an argument because it shifts the focus inward and reminds your partner that you care.

4. Remember a phrase, poem, song, or saying that is soothing and use it repeatedly so it becomes like a hypnotic cue. I use "The Lord is my shepherd, I shall not want" or internally hear Louis Armstrong singing "What a Wonderful World." Other phrases people use: "Everything is love," "This too shall pass," "I get to make mistakes." Find a phrase that fits for you, and practice during the week. Take a moment to breathe deeply and say the phrase until you feel your body calming. Then imagine a small frustration and say the soothing phrase. Over time, this will become an instant relaxation potion.

5. Imagine both of you in the "us" place. This technique comes from Ken Keyes. If you are feeling angry and blaming your part-ner, use the phrase "One of *us*." One of *us* is being obnoxious. One of *us* is afraid. One of *us* doesn't understand. One of *us* is upset and frustrated. Do it for both of you. It could be either of us who's having any of these feelings. Put an imaginary circle around both of you and stay mentally in the "us" place. You don't have to deny your feelings or that your partner is being

difficult (maybe you are, too), but simply stay in the "us" place so you don't make separation between you.

6. Imagine a circle of light surrounding everyone involved in the conflict or pain—the light of "us" together in this.

7. Check out your interpretations. Ask yourself the following: "What did my partner really say verbatim?" Or "What meaning am I attributing to his or her words?"

8. Ask yourself, "How old am I acting?" Then smile at that little part of yourself and say, I understand. It makes sense considering your past, but that was then, this is now. "It's okay. I'm forty-seven and I can handle this."

9. Say, I get to make mistakes. If you start feeling shame or fear, say to yourself, "I get to make mistakes. Everyone makes mistakes. I'm not bad."

10. Go into "big mind." This is a teaching that comes from Buddhism. Instead of focusing on *my* hurt, *my* irritation, *my* fear, *our* troubled relationship, say to yourself, "I am feeling *the* hurt, *the* fear, *the* confusion common to most relationships." These are natural human emotions that many other people are feeling right this moment. You are not alone and you are feeling what most people have felt.

11. Instead of saying "I'm mad at you," say meyouanger or meyoufight. This is a suggestion by Joko Beck in *Everyday Zen: Love and Work*. It shifts the struggle from I versus You to meyoufight—we're all tangled up in this. It's one thing.

What to Do If You Take a Break

12. Observe your fight as if you were seeing it on a movie screen. Watch with fascination and interest. Can you see that you and your partner are just playing out your parts? Is the conversation

predictable, even funny? Could you easily play each other's part? How would you like to rewrite the script? Now imagine you are watching the scene on a movie screen in five years. Ten years. How serious does it feel then? Then imagine the scene with you acting differently.

13. Distract yourself. If you feel intense and can't stop replaying a scene, refocus. Take the dead leaves off your plants, put the dishes away, sweep a floor, watch TV, play a musical instrument, take a shower, sing, nap, rent a movie, take a walk, go shopping and look for some small thing.

14. Call a trusted friend who has a sense of humor and who can help you gain perspective on the problem and see your part. Don't call someone who will feel sorry for you.

15. Remember the big picture. If you are feeling discouraged about your relationship, imagine for a moment flying over all the people within a hundred miles of you. How many are going through an argument similar to yours right this moment, or this week? Hundreds? Thousands? Millions? Again remember you are not alone in your experience.

16. Write in a journal. Sit down and let the feelings, thoughts, and ideas flow out of you. Don't censor. Just let yourself say everything that comes to you. Often you will start to feel lighter and have a new perspective.

17. Practice Tonglin meditation. Tonglin is a very powerful form of meditation that can help a person deal immediately with a troubling situation. I spoke about Tonglin in my previous book, *If the Buddha Dated,* and numerous people responded that it had been extremely helpful. It can be done in various stages.

If you are feeling hurt, scared, or panicked, the first step is to breathe in the feeling, experience it, and breathe out light energy and good wishes. Next, imagine taking in the feelings of your partner and sending out a blessing and light energy. You can do this for yourself, your partner, and for your relationship. The third step is to think of all the other people suffering the same struggle and pain as you are. Again, breathe in the emotions, and breathe out lovingkindness and a beam of light for all of them. The idea is that when you come into unity and oneness with others, often the sense of separation dissolves along with the feelings of anger and hurt. In this way, we can take an active step to connect and transcend the ego-backed emotions of hurt, righteousness, and anger. A couple can do this together. If you are embroiled in a fight, sit together, breathe in the frustration of both of you, and breathe out a blessing and good wishes for your relationship.

18. Seek counseling. If you can't seem to calm yourself or self-soothe after making a concerted effort, consider getting professional help.

You can experiment with any of these approaches to self-soothing. Some may work; others may not connect for you. Pick one or two and use them consistently, or find others that help. For one man, the question "How old am I?" was like an instant key to shifting his awareness of a situation, and calming himself. Over time, as you develop the capacity to calm yourself, you will find that you can step back, be less reactive, and the situation won't seem so big or ominous.

47 MORE CLARITY, MORE LOVE: HELP A GOOD RELATIONSHIP GET BETTER

Jessie and Dan considered their marriage solid and loving. They were successful professionals with two children, a good balance between shared interests and separate endeavors. They were active in their Quaker community and thoroughly enjoyed each other's company. So it came as something of a surprise to Dan when Jessie said she wanted them to go to a weekend Quaker couples' enrichment retreat in a nearby city. Dan agreed, but commented on the drive to the workshop, "This will be a piece of cake."

With a self-deprecating laugh, Dan said, "Within five minutes of the first process, I was crying intensely about my father. I had no idea how much pain I was carrying around about him. I had thought it was all resolved."

The impact of the workshop on both Jessie and Dan was so powerful that they decided to train to become facilitators. "I thought we had a good relationship, but since we've learned to process conflict in a deeper way, it's become so much better."

"I think most people push things away without even knowing it," Jessie said. "They don't know how, or don't have a concept of how good a relationship can be. Layers and layers of things don't get taken care of. People are lonely and distant, but they don't really know it. We didn't know it. We almost look forward to having conflicts to settle because it has become a very intimate process, and we feel so close afterward."

I asked if there was often something to process between them.

Jessie said, "It's amazing that we don't run out of things to talk about, but life keeps changing. For example, our daughter left for college and I wanted Dan to be home for supper more, because without her around, I felt lonely."

Dan interjected, "The conversation might start with me saying that I don't look forward to dinner because it was so contentious when I was a child. Then I listen to Jessie and hear how much it means to her. I tell myself not to stay stuck in the past. And we keep listening."

"So what happened?" I asked.

"I have been coming home more now," Dan said, turning to Jessie. "Have you noticed?"

"Yes, but what's more important is that by talking about it, and being understood, it doesn't seem like such a big problem. Often we find that these situations just ease. We both give, we both accept each other."

The interview drifted to their sexual relationship. They both smiled with that telltale look that I have so often seen with loving couples. "After clearing the air, we feel so close to each other we sometimes make love for hours," she added. "That's something we'd never done before, in twenty years of marriage."

While the retreats include a variety of experiences, the heart of the process is a simple listening exercise very much like the one I touched upon in the previous section. Each partner sits facing the other. Then one person has the floor or, more accurately, holds a pillow or talking stick. She brings up a concern to be aired and talks about both the situation and her feelings, speaking one or two sentences at a time, which the listener repeats. If the speaker feels misunderstood, she can repeat what was said. If the listener blanks out or forgets, he can ask the speaker to repeat what she said.

What is quite extraordinary is that solely by listening deeply with the intention of understanding, relationships can change. Many couples say that this exercise was the first time they felt they could relax and talk, because they knew they weren't going to be interrupted or countered. Once people have felt deeply cared-for and understood, solutions often come easier.

When we bring understanding, kindness, and devotion to our relationship by addressing conflicts, fear starts to melt because there's nothing left to hide—no secrets or shame. Our bond becomes supple and strong and we can move beyond thoughts to that place beyond ideas where we meet in the heart of the beloved.

PART EIGHT

MAKING LOVE WITH THE BELOVED

48 MAKING LOVE: THE UNION OF BODY AND SPIRIT

Those who don't feel this Love
pulling them like a river,
those who don't drink dawn
like a cup of springwater
or take in sunset like supper,
those who don't want to change,
let them sleep.

This Love is beyond the study of theology . . .
I've given up on my brain
I've torn the cloth to shreds
and thrown it away

—*Rumi,* LIKE THIS

After spending several years as an ascetic, Buddha decided that the extremes of self-denial and sensuous gratification were both misdirected. Instead, he chose the Middle Way—a path of balance, responsibility, and clarity. And although Buddha was celibate, as were most of his early followers, we can still draw on his principles of lovingkindness, nonviolence, clear seeing, mindfulness, and good intentions to provide a foundation for enduring sexual relationships.

Sexuality in the heart of the beloved is about breaking our shells and experiencing ourselves beyond words. It is an intricate intermingling of spirit and body, of bringing our lives into a meaningful whole—a union of commitment, passion, joy, humor, kindness, knowing, and honesty. The sexual bond becomes an expression of all we are—physical love within the union or context of all we mean to each other.

Sadly, however, this is not always the case. For some couples, lovemaking is a physical act devoid of tenderness, pleasure, and human connection. It's something a woman does for her man, because, well, she's married, and it's her duty. The concepts of pleasure, connection, giving and receiving, and dissolving into the arms of your beloved are foreign.

In talking with numerous people about sexuality, I have heard everything from "He does it in seven minutes" to "She always has a headache and never wants it" or "I don't care if I ever have sex again." Fortunately, there are also couples who, after twenty years, can say, "We make love for hours and it just keeps getting better" or "In forty years, I don't think two weeks have ever gone by without making love—it brings us close, it makes life easier. Life wouldn't seem the same without it."

Consider these words from Stephen and Ondrea Levine, authors of *Embracing the Beloved*:

> *There is nothing like making love with the Beloved. Nothing like the boundaryless heart to make us edgeless and agile. Making love in the shared body is the natural expression of living in the shared heart. Such boundaryless interaction is called "sacred sexuality." Touch sending waves of energy through the body/mind into the spirit . . .*

These words and thoughts are beautiful. Yet it's important not to separate sacred sexuality from bodies, arousal, smells, moaning, excitement, and pleasure. Sexuality that endures for couples is both an intensely physical experience *and* a deeply felt expression of knowing, loving, caring, and devotion.

Accepting the very fact that sexuality can lead to a powerful expansion of energy, and bring intense pleasure and delight, is to accept the wondrous nature of our earthly bodies. It is the lightning, thunder, and budding flowers that live within us. When two people in a caring relationship allow the full power of their sexuality to unfold together it can be intensely intimate and intertwined with the spiritual path. By opening ourselves fully to each other, we also open ourselves to the wonder of all creation.

Of course, the rhythm, expression, and intensity of making love varies with different couples and different times. Some have sustained a continuous sexual relationship for over forty years that nearly always brought pleasure. For others, sexuality was problematic at first but became more open and spontaneous with time. For many more, there was a waxing and waning of sexual desire, based on times of change, having young children, conflict in the relationship, aging, or sometimes for inexplicable reasons.

Overall, though, three patterns did emerge over the course of my interviews with long-term couples. First, there were those for whom sexuality was like a healing glue. If the couple had been at odds, making love broke through the separateness and brought them back together. Then there were those who said they needed to feel very clear and loving *before* they could be sexual. And then there were others still, who said sexuality had a circular effect—making love brought them closer, and talking and clearing out conflict kindled their sexual desire. I should also add a fourth category here—the mixed roles. Namely, in several relationships, the man said that making love helped him feel close so he could better talk things over, while his partner wanted to clear out conflict before making love.

I was repeatedly in awe of people's willingness and ability to talk about their sexual relationships. This area that we so often avoid is incredibly rich both emotionally and spiritually. The following quotes bring together many of the important elements in sustaining a bonded sexual relationship. Those I quote include people with various spiritual backgrounds, including Buddhist, Christian, and Sufi.

Marianne, who was part of a Sufi group, spoke of her experience in her marriage of seven years:

"I've learned the hard way that there must be a personal connection. Early in the sexual revolution, when I had a strong sexual drive, I plunged into relationships not knowing much about my body or the meaning of sex. I would reach a deep, intense connection whenever I made love, and suddenly feel intricately involved with the person and get trapped in situations that weren't good. If my sexual partner couldn't meet me at that deep level, it was shattering. I was left vulnerable and open with no one to meet me there. I've had to reverse my engines and go about getting to know the person first.

"With Phillip, my husband and partner, we spent a lot of time getting to know each other and made a commitment before we were sexual. This made it possible to be at a deep level together from the start. For me, it's not been an easy road. Being open stirs stuff up—the past, fears, and whatever has not been said between us. That's why the bottom line is a deep vulnerability that permeates everything in our lives. In spite of the fact that it's gone up and down over the years, there's never been the threat of someone leaving or going out on the other. There is a lot of other glue in our relationship—we have a deep level of commitment that lives inside us and holds us together. It's not that we have to make an effort—the commitment is just there. Phillip is about as true-blue as you can get. And we are both completely loyal.

"We're pretty cautious about deciding to make love because if it's not going to be good emotionally and spiritually, we end up thinking, 'Oh God, why did I do that? I'd rather read a book.' It could be physically very satisfying, but I end up feeling separated and empty. I need everything cleared out first so I'm in a centered state. Then it's great. When we meet in that deep way and feel clear, then it's lovely and worth doing. It's an elevated state that has a certain harmony—a doorway to an experience of something powerful and bigger—like being one with everything. It requires a lot of self-awareness to make love at that level."

In contrast with Marianne and Phillip, some couples can nearly always connect easily through sex. This is a gift that cannot be made to happen; it's about a deep physical attraction that is biological as well as emotional. Elaine, who met her husband, Roger, while still in high school, waited until marriage to be sexual. "We went together for three years, and were not sexual until we married—there were strong prohibitions against that, and we were concerned about an unwanted pregnancy. But there was always an attraction. We have been through so much—my undiagnosed depression, our daughter's chronic life-threatening illness, and all the angry words that flew because we were afraid and didn't know what to do about our daughter. But, through it all, we are always able to come back together, to comfort each other and talk things over. We've always saved Friday night for our special movie date together. And we still make love."

I asked her if their sexual relationship had changed much. Her eyes shone and there was a smile in her voice when she said, "The desire is still there; it's always been there. I would say Roger is a very good lover, and he always has been. We married when I was twenty, and sex was good from the beginning. It seems completely natural, biological. Some things just never change."

Ruth spoke about the role of sexuality throughout her thirty-eight-year marriage that she described as a blessing. Her words, which come from a Christian tradition, encapsulate the melding of sexuality, spirituality, and lovingkindness.

"With sexuality, there is something that goes on between the spirit and the soul and the physical—an element that wants to give and take, to understand. The sexual relationship happens because of love. Real love that comes from giving, knowing, and sharing. It's not an emotional, sentimental thing. Love follows when you show care, respect, and kindness. Sexuality is like a circle: the sexual union builds the love and the love builds the sexual desire. Sexuality binds us together. With a successful sexual relationship, there is a delight in each other that filters through the day. It's an incredible superglue.

"There is something magical in the commitment to leave our father and mother and cleave to our partner. To truly become as one. When you have a commitment that is for life, and there is a backing of spirituality—love is patient, kind, and forgiving—you have an ointment that soothes.

"Without commitment, sex is like opening up a box of chocolates—a sweet taste but no meaning. With dissatisfaction in a sexual relationship, something wears away—the relationship rusts, and the harmony fades.

"But with that lifelong commitment to love and know each other, sexuality builds and builds, way beyond any fantasy a teenager could dream of."

Paul and Haley no longer are explicitly sexual because of aging (Paul is eighty-seven), but to be with them is to be with lovers. Haley commented, "Now I know my worst enemy is gravity, but Paul still thinks I'm a beauty. He still calls me his darling, his special one. I see the love in his eyes. I know he'll never leave and he knows I'll never leave him. We are together in every way." They make love throughout the day, with touches, playfulness, glances, and kind words.

Many of the couples I've spoken with, no matter what their religion or spiritual beliefs, or sexual affinity, said in various ways that commitment, vulnerability, trust, honesty, and love were the foundations of a pleasure-filled and enduring sexual relationship.

49 SEXUAL HIGH OR SEXUAL CONNECTION: WHAT'S THE DIFFERENCE?

To the extent that you are addicted to getting high you will never be able to enjoy a conjugal relationship. A high is like a rush; love is like letting the water bubble up and flow over us and through us.
—Sigurd Hoppe, psychotherapist

How do we understand sexuality in the context of Buddhist teachings, which maintain that desire is a hindrance to spirituality because it kindles attachments? Is desire always an attachment? We can make some distinctions . . . between sexual desire for a "high" and sexual desire in the context of a loving relationship. I think we'd be deluding ourselves to say that sexuality does not include desire. We are hardwired as a species to be sexually attracted, fall in love, and procreate. This is the animal side of our sexuality. We add a spiritual quality when sexual desire and excitement are embedded in a loving relationship where we come together, eyes open to each other, and mutually take pleasure in giving, receiving, knowing, and being close to each other. Being sexual in the present with our beloved, without expectations or ego, is worlds apart from using ego-centered sex for physical stimulation, a high, or shoring up our sense of worth.

The Sufi poet Rumi intertwines sensuous images of lovers, the beloved, and nature: "The sky bares its neck so beautifully," or "We're here again with the Beloved. This air, a shout. These meadow sounds, an astonishing myth," or "Inside this globe the soul roars like thunder, And now Silence . . ."

Sexuality in the heart of the beloved is a natural, free-flowing experience—a mutual coming-together of two committed people, heart, mind, spirit, body. If we can empty our mind and welcome the meadow sounds, thunder, silence, and air into our lovemaking, we can dissolve into the experience, and feel great joy in our union.

This is not easy for many. Sexuality without attachments is extremely alien to a Western mind brought up in a culture that teaches us to fixate on acquiring, owning, possessing, controlling, and getting what we want, sometimes at the expense of others or by sacrificing our values. But it is a shift we need to make so we enter into a flow of conjugal love, where giving and receiving merge into a single dance without expectations and images.

Sexuality *with* attachments becomes an I-object experience. As Paul Pearsall writes, "If we have sex to seek variety, challenge, and conquest it is our biology rather than our spirit and consciousness which is directing us." And speaking of biology, many people equate sex with orgasm. It's a high, a tension release, an intense physical sensation. But orgasm is orgasm, just a tiny moment in time, no matter how pleasurable. If sex becomes focused on this momentary high, separate from our partner, separate from pleasuring one another, separate from relationship, we render both of us into objects. Emptiness will follow—an emptiness that can never be filled with sex, no matter how many times we try; no matter how intense the orgasm; no matter how many different partners we have; no matter how many gizmos we use or books we read.

I-object sexuality has a quality of needing, taking, expecting, or grasping. It can be very subtle. For example, a man who equates sex with his self-worth may mask his neediness by appearing to pleasure his partner. But it has the quality of playing her like a violin so he can meet his needs. It's a disguised kind of using behavior that can appear as care, but the motivation is self-gratification.

When we are in an I-object mode of relating, our mind may be deluged with thoughts such as: "Am I doing it right?" "Does he love me?" "Will I get what I want?" Sometimes, we simply shut down and feel lost, or we look at the ceiling and hope it will soon be over. Other times, we may have intense physical feelings, and feel a glow for a while, but the gnawing emptiness creeps back and once again we're on the quest for sex or something to fill that emptiness. Remember, when we don't know how to feel deeply connected or experience intimacy, we often seek stimulation or a "high."

Sex that is about a high, and has absolutely nothing to do with relationship or coming into awareness of who you are. To use another's body without connecting to that person in a knowing, loving way is to create a violation that penetrates all of our being. *We may not understand or acknowledge the cost, but we experience it in our feelings of loneliness, emptiness, and restlessness.* The cost may also be experienced through a variety of compulsions or addictions. This can even be between good and caring people, who simply don't know any other way.

I spoke with colleague Sigurd Hoppe, who specializes in sex addiction and male sexuality.

Many men feel a vacuum—there is no real fulfillment, no inti-
macy, only the using of a woman (or another man) as an ob-
ject. At any level, to indulge oneself at the expense of another is
exploitation. We end up feeling cheated, empty. We rage inside
and often lash out at our partner—holding her/him responsible
for the emptiness we feel as a result of our using. We may sub-
merge our anger with alcohol or other drugs. We come away
truly empty, feeling crummy, or shameful. Nothing ever satis-
fies. Using behavior only empties us further. It's like trying to
fill up the emptiness of the soul by getting high, but it is
actually a profound experience in emptying the soul, or
emptying oneself. *For men, there are so many layers of self-*
defense that have to be overcome to have relatedness.

Which takes me to the subject of pornography, which has
increasingly become an interloper into relationships. Over and
over, I find that when there are sexual difficulties, the use of
pornography is lurking in the closet. I asked my friend Larry, who
had been in various men's consciousness-raising groups, to explain why men like pornography. He said:

With pornography, you have complete control. There is no real
human being at the other end of the relationship. You can go
into a fantasy world and create any relationship you want. You
can do things to her, use her, and have no regard for her needs.
There is no connection, no reality, and no challenge to be hu-
man or deal with anything that is human. The person in that
picture is simply an object.

We can't compartmentalize consciousness. Buddhism is totally
about kindness and respect for all people and seeing the intercon-

nection between all things. For example, when we look at a woman in a pornographic image, do we also think of what might have led her to be there? Incest? Abuse? Poverty? Would we want our mother, sister, or daughter to be in such pictures? Are we really willing to participate in her subjugation? Do we want those images dwelling in our minds?

Many women have spoken to me of the rage they feel when they come upon their partner looking at pornography on the Internet. "I feel so upset," one woman said. "How can he go from looking at that to making love with me? I lose all desire to be with him. I wonder what is going on in his mind." Not all women feel as she does. However, while men and women may not know the harmful effects of looking at pornography consciously, they experience it in the lack of depth and surrender in their sexual lives. They experience it in their difficulty engaging with an imperfect flesh-and-blood partner—with being open, engaged, honest, and loving.

The use of pornography, while predominantly by men, also extends to women, but often in a different form. Women sometimes sexually objectify themselves in appearance and behavior to feel a sense of power or control. Other times, in an attempt to please their partner, they go along with sexual practices they don't like. Some women go into chat rooms and create fantasy relationships when they are angry at their partner, or to ease feelings of loneliness.

In helping men explore their underlying motivation for using pornography, I found the patterns often started with an awkward adolescent who felt terrified of "girls." One man said, "I had never kissed a girl by my senior year in high school, and I thought about it all the time but I was too scared to ask anyone out. *Playboy* became my outlet."

The path out of this dilemma for men and women is to make a leap of faith and commit to moving beyond any form of I-object sexual behavior. As part of Buddhist practice, people often commit to give up something they use for an escape for a period of months. This is done in the spirit of exploration to find out what arises when they let go of their escape hatches. It could be sugar, chocolate, gambling, talking behind someone's back, being late to work, alcohol, or . . . pornography.

There are many people who need to make friends with that awkward adolescent inside, to help him or her grow up into the adult, the lover, and the friend. We need to focus on our feelings and fears so we can free ourselves to form an emotionally intimate, human connection, where sexuality is a full and rich experience that deepens our knowing and our love.

5Ø FINDING OUT WHY THE FIRE HAS FADED

When sexual desire and attraction wane or disappear, something sweet and important is lost. I hasten to add that as people age, sexual arousal sometimes becomes problematic or the desire simply fades. This still does not preclude a loving physical connection.

I urge couples who have lost their spark and desire to explore what has created the separation. Sometimes, couples attempt to rationalize sexual distance with comments such as: "We have become companions" or "It's natural that you lose sexual interest with children." Maybe so, for a little while, but the real reasons are usually deeper. The loss of sexuality in a relationship can dull the vitality and create separation. It heightens the risk of creating an emotional chasm, or someone having an affair.

As you read through the following list of possible reasons for loss of sexual interest, tune in to your physical and emotional reactions. They are the best indicator of what's true for you.

1. Medications, physical illness, depression, and anxiety. Check with your doctor or naturopath to see if this is possible.

2. Lack of knowledge about sex, sexual arousal, and the possibilities of sexual union. The partners care about each other, but sex is primarily a physical act that lacks a deeper meaning because it is focused on orgasm. It can be helpful to read a book on sexuality, go to sexuality workshops, talk with other couples, or possibly go to a counselor. One step is simply to take more time to touch, caress, and become deeply acquainted with each other's bodies.

3. The relationship has lost its meaning. Complacency has set in and the couple isn't talking, spending time together, and making the relationship a priority. It may also mean that the individuals' lives are in a rut and there is little joy, creativity, spontaneity, and pleasure in life in general.

4. One or both people have been having sex out of duty because they are afraid to say no. Going against the flow of one's truths has created an inner resistance that dulls the desire to be sexual.

5. There is a covert form of "using" underlying the sexual relationship. If either person is using sex to fulfill a need for a physical high, for security, as a tension release, to vent feelings of anxiety, or to shore up the ego, it's like toxins creeping into the relationship.

6. Developmental stages have been blocked. For example, if someone is primarily in a teenage rebellious state, he or she is not likely to be emotionally generous with their lovemaking because giving to another feels like losing a part of oneself. In another situation, if the two people are making love out of a dependent child state, they are using sex to fulfill an emotional emptiness. This might result in feeling disturbed inside, sad, or having sudden flashes of anger at one's partner.

7. There are unresolved issues of sexual abuse or misuse from the past. There may be a need to reflect on sexual messages from family and culture, or earlier sexual abuse, to see if there are wounds that are unconsciously triggering the nervous system to perceive the current situation as dangerous or harmful. For some, this exploration will require the help of a skilled therapist or counselor.

8. If sex has been paired with promiscuity, pornography, putting notches on the belt, or shame, some people find it difficult to be sexual within marriage. As one man said, "We've had a nearly celibate relationship. I constantly have the thought, 'I can't have sex with her, she's my wife. I love her and sex is dirty.' "

9. Hormonal changes related to age and/or menopause. This varies immensely and there are some remedies that help people maintain sexual desire.

10. Pregnancy and the birth of a child.

If any of these ideas apply to you or your relationship, the next step is to consider what steps you can take to make changes in your life so that you can again feel the sweetness of making love in the arms of the beloved.

51 DEEPEN YOUR SEXUAL BOND

There is some kiss we want
with our whole lives,
the touch of Spirit on the body . . .

At night I open the window
and ask the moon to come
and press its face against mine.

Breathe into me.
                    —*Rumi,* LIKE THIS

Sometimes, improving a sexual relationship requires learning more about sexuality and the physical body. Other times, the sexual problem is a relationship problem that can be helped by becoming better helpmates and being more open with each other.

Sometimes, we are faced with dismantling all the messages we've gotten about sex as it relates to power, control, domination, security, and duty. Whatever reasons resonate with you, the first steps are to reaffirm your commitment to each other, name the difficulties, and reveal your true feelings. Remember: The amount of sex you have is not as important as the level of connection you make and the pleasure you feel.

Here are some ideas that might help you on your journey, whether sex feels obsessive or there is a loss of desire:

1. Be willing to know yourself deeply. A first step can be to say, "I am willing to feel whatever is happening inside me throughout the day, during sex, or when thinking about sex. I am willing to reflect on myself, to meet whatever is hiding."

2. Become open and vulnerable to your partner—talk about fears, hopes, grief, and joy. Talk about your sexual relationship and ask your partner how she or he feels about it. What are his or her reactions or feelings? Be absolutely honest with each other. Talk about how long it takes you to become aroused, and ne-gotiate how to handle that.

3. Tune in to your motivation for being sexual. Notice if you are using sex for a physical high, to fulfill a need, release tension, be dutiful, please your partner, convince yourself you are loved, or avoid conflict with your partner. If you are sexual at these times, notice how it feels—before, during, and after. Explore ways to be intimate emotionally without sex. Also explore touching, massaging, and pleasuring each other without focus-ing on orgasm—or even becoming sexual.

4. When you are sexual, go very slowly, take at least thirty to forty-five minutes to pleasure each other and explore each other's bodies. Allow the expansive energy to move upward into your heart. Remember, women usually need more time to be aroused than men.

5. When you are sexual, allow the energy to build. Breathe it up-ward and become willing to experience the power of its energy along with feelings of joy and intense pleasure. This may sound easy, but surrendering to powerful physical pleasure often col-lides with the image of being a "nice girl" or "nice guy" or feel-ing the threat of being too exposed and vulnerable.

6. Take turns giving and receiving. One can be the receiver and say exactly what he or she wants. Then trade roles.

7. Explore the ways in which you take good care of yourself in the whole of your life—healthy eating, exercise, meeting new people, exploring your interests, stretching your capabilities, being of service, becoming more conscious and aware. The idea is to bring yourself to a relationship as a fully functioning human being, committed to your own journey.

8. Put away pornography in all forms. Remember, I-object thinking internally divides you and often translates into I-object behavior. If this is difficult or you find you are unable to do so, you may need a support group or professional help.

9. Refrain from alcohol or other drugs, particularly before being sexual. Ask yourself, "How is sober sex different from sex with the use of alcohol and other drugs?"

10. Be willing to stretch your edges. Take a shower first and rub oil on each other. Wash each other's feet. Make eye contact during sex, say each other's names, tune in deeper to your partner's subtle reactions. Guide your partner's hands. Take turns giving and receiving. Change the rhythm, the way you touch and move. Have candles, soft lighting, something that smells good to you, soft music you both like. Prior to making love, talk about what you enjoy and what you would like to have different.

11. Make love throughout the day by touching, being playful, listening, and taking a full part in all facets of your relationship. When you say to your partner, "What can I do for you today?" and follow through, you are making love in a wonderful way.

12. If you repeatedly have a hard time responding, feeling sexual, or become flooded by past painful memories, get professional help.

If you take these suggestions to heart, and even do a few of them, you are likely to notice changes in yourself and your relationship. Sometimes, improving a sexual relationship is not complicated; other times, there may be underlying concerns to explore.

Sexuality is woven together with our physical, mental, and emotional well-being. Our sexual energy is one with our life energy and our spiritual energy. When we can come into full relationship with our beloved, we are healing all of who we are.

52 SUPPORT EACH OTHER BEING COMPLETELY HONEST

When I am a willow tree, I can be with another and can still stand my ground—I don't change and become a different kind of tree just to please the other. I stand as myself even when the other pushes up against me. But I can bend when I want to, and I can grow when I need to.

—Janet Luhrs, SIMPLE LOVING

On the spiritual path, we move toward the edge of our fears, and leap beyond our egos so we can meet in union, love, and delight. This often necessitates a clearing process of old messages that keep us from being honest.

When we are sexual out of guilt, duty, or to keep someone from leaving, we are etching a message in our brain that pairs sex with self-betrayal. We become divided. Women in particular often talk about the nagging thought "I don't want to" running through their minds, accompanied by guilt for not being a good or pleasing partner. As a result, a woman may say a halfhearted yes to sex, comply, and have an empty sexual experience, which then builds up greater resistance to being sexual.

If we can remember that our current generation is only beginning to move beyond thousands of years of a basic marriage barter that included women being sexually available at all times in exchange for the illusion of security, we can understand this inner struggle and confusion. It is extremely common.

Women need to be encouraged to say no to sex without being guilted or shamed. This opens the door to saying yes. Here is the story of a woman who made a fearless leap into honesty, and in doing so healed a troubled sexual relationship.

Marie talked about a dramatic shift in her sexual relationship with her partner in the seventh year of their marriage:

"Early in our relationship I wasn't present when we were sexual. My mind would wander and I'd feel shut down. It was more about performance than intimacy. Lawrence would notice it. But I didn't know what to do. Then I read an article about rape in marriage and it set my mind to thinking. I always had this feeling 'I don't want to' in the back of my mind, even though when I said yes, it was physically pleasurable.

"I finally realized I never felt I could say no to Lawrence without him pouting or giving me a pained look—or both. I realized my fear of saying no was a reenactment of the sexual abuse by my grandfather—I could never say no to him. I felt incredibly confused because he was kind and gentle and it actually felt good, but it also felt very wrong.

"Because of the trust in our marriage, I was able to explain this to Lawrence. 'I need to be able to say no to you and have you completely accept it. It doesn't mean I don't want to be sexual with you, because I do. But I want you to come on to me a lot so I can practice saying no. I've got to know I can do that. If you're willing to do this for me, I'm willing to listen to your frustration and hurt."

"What was his response?" I asked.

"He didn't get it."

"What did you do?"

"I said to him, 'Lawrence, we have three daughters and whatever we do will filter down to them. Do you want them to be sexual in high school or with some guy they don't really like because they don't feel they can say no?'"

"What did he say to that?" I asked.

"He got it!" She laughed.

Lawrence then entered the conversation: "I finally understood how important it was, but I had to get past the idea that she was rejecting me—that my worth was measured by her saying yes when I wanted sex. But it was better afterward. Now when we are sexual we're both really there. There are no sneaky aspects about sex. It's more about quality than quantity."

Marie added, "We could go through this because we had so much trust in each other and such a strong connection. It takes a long time to establish that level of trust. I also realized that I wanted Lawrence to ask me directly to be sexual so I could say a clear yes. I wanted to get totally away from any form of manipulation or assumptions about Lawrence having a right to me. When he started asking me directly it made a tremendous difference."

After a pause in the conversation, I asked, "That change happened almost ten years ago. How is your sex life now?"

Lawrence averted his eyes, and Marie's face shone bright. "The best ever," she said. "It's always the best. Lawrence is a wonderful lover. I always feel so well taken care of."

"I'm embarrassed," Lawrence added, with a smile.

"How is it for you?" I asked him.

He smiled. "If I had it my way we'd have sex more often," he said. "I usually wait for Marie to initiate because that way she's really into it. I also think that making love can be very healing when things are a little off. It can help me open up. But Marie doesn't always feel that way. She wants things to be clear between us before we are sexual. And sometimes that's right, too. You can never know for sure. There aren't any fixed rules."

If women have received the cultural message that they aren't supposed to thoroughly enjoy sex but they must say yes, men have been conditioned to think they should have sex whenever it's available. But as men become conscious, they, too, want sex in the context of care and connection and must feel absolutely free to say yes or no to being sexual.

Part of everyone's evolution is to be clear when we come together to make love. That we bring our mind, body, and spirit into the "us" place, to mutually express love, pleasure each other, and feel at one.

53 STAY LOVERS DURING THE PARENTING YEARS

There is nothing quite so dramatic as the time when you become a parent. From the moment of knowing you are pregnant, to the birth itself, to the dynamic shift that takes place the day the baby comes home, any parent will tell you that a newborn changes every aspect of your life. This includes your sexual relationship.

Sustaining romance through parenthood is one of the first and most difficult tests of a long-term relationship. I asked Marie and

Lawrence how they managed to maintain their sexual union over the years with three daughters.

"We sometimes make dates to make love on a Friday or Saturday," Marie said. "We make sure to have time for each other at least once a week whether it's being sexual or just having time together. We make a big effort not to let our children come between making time for ourselves, even though we do a lot with the kids."

Her response was common to the couples I interviewed who maintained a vital sexual relationship even with children, work, and other obligations. Their relationship as lovers and partners remained paramount. The same was true for Charles and Elizabeth, who had blushingly described their relationship of forty-six years as "pretty torrid." When I asked about children, jobs, and other obligations, they responded, "We never let that get in the way."

Ruth, whom I mentioned earlier, said, "Sex was wonderful during the time I was nursing our three children. I think he liked that there was milk in my breasts. *There was always our relationship separate from being parents.*"

A crucial element of keeping sexual desire alive during the first year of parenthood is that the partner be supportive of the mother—to give to her, adore her, and care for her. This keeps the romance alive. If the mother feels constantly exhausted, and does not feel supported or appreciated, resentments may start to build or she may just be too exhausted to care. So, even though your partner becomes a mother, it's important to continue treating her as your sweetheart and lover.

This leads me to the next point. It is crucial that the level of intimacy between adult partners remains strong and that there be a clear separation between parents and children. In troubled marriages, often one or both parents meet their needs for emotional closeness through a child, to the exclusion of their partner.

When we make a child our primary source of closeness or intimacy, the child becomes caught in a triangle, unconsciously torn between feeling special and worrying about the parent who has been excluded. The child may also feel a sense of failure, because she cannot fulfill her parents' need for intimacy or assuage their emptiness.

I have often heard couples who come for therapy comment that their lives are too busy for making love. I would suggest, though, that the true reasons almost always go deeper. In nearly all the successful relationships from my interviews, couples made dates with each other in the midst of demanding jobs, children, responsibilities, and service to the community. It wasn't just a date for sex, it was a time to find pleasure and delight in being together, to kindle and rekindle the attraction and desire for each other.

54 UNDERSTAND THE TRUE MEANING OF MONOGAMY

To immerse ourselves deeply into love and sexual union, it is usually wise to be monogamous. This gives us the freedom of completely knowing another person, of developing a rhythm of day-to-day experience that braids our lives together in the shared heart that can take us into the shared body.

This is in no way a moral judgment. But having been part of the sexually permissive sixties and early seventies, and having talked to many couples who have attempted "open marriages," my observation is this: if we want to dissolve into the arms of the beloved, to experience that mystical union, we need the safety and depth of monogamy. This doesn't mean that we might not feel great love for other people, but negotiating two sexual relationships simultaneously is very problematic.

Too often, people wanting "open marriage," or to be "polyamorous," to use a current term, are either attempting to meet unrecognized emotional needs through sex, fill some nameless emptiness, or use the additional relationship to avoid facing whatever is missing in their primary relationship. I have seen only a few exceptions when these arrangements didn't lead to stress, confusion, or disappointment. Very often in these relationships, there is an enormous amount of time focused on sex and the ensuing emotional turmoil that can arise from such arrangements. In many cases, there is also a lot of alcohol, marijuana, and other drugs.

Sexuality in the heart of the beloved is about complete surrender to that person, to being connected at the deepest possible level. We become as one, which reflects our union with God, or Spirit. When we create that special union with another person, it becomes something to treasure.

I spoke with my Sufi teacher Zamila about this subject. She said:

We're all trying to become whole. That's why we go into relationships. The whole reason to be monogamous is that whenever you enter someone's field you are entering into their essence. Every time we go into the essence of another person, we create a shared essence with the partner. We become one body. This is a very deep thing. If we do it on a sexual level, we are mixing essences at the deepest possible level. If we bring an-

*other being in there we are polluting that essence. People don't
know how deep intimacy can truly go.*

Several people alluded to similar thoughts in our interviews.
They spoke of becoming so much at one with their partner, of
mingling with that person at every level of his or her being, that
to intrude on that oneness would feel totally unthinkable. Other
people said more earthly things, such as, I wouldn't want all the
confusion. I can't imagine there wouldn't be hurt and jealousy. I
can barely handle one relationship.

Ultimately monogamy opens the possibility of going deeply
into the meaning of union and feeling in harmony with All
That Is.

<hr />

55 WHAT TO DO WITH ATTRACTION TO OTHERS

It is natural to feel attracted to people other than your mate. Indeed, as our love becomes more boundless, we often feel intense
warmth, affection, and care for others and sometimes it crosses
the line into sexual attraction. Keeping this boundary clear is the
task of a committed monogamous relationship. For some this is
easy, for others it is not.

For Eric, the line was absolute, and it had never been crossed.
"Of course I've felt attracted to other women, but I'm married to
my wife, and I would never consider it or risk the harm and the
hurt it would cause."

Usually, when there is a serious flirtation or an affair, there has
been a long period of dwindling satisfaction in a relationship.

Lily and Les survived a near affair on the part of Lily. Their sexual relationship had been problematic throughout their fifteen-year marriage.

Lily said, "I have this thing about holding back, not being able to open up. A couple of years after my first daughter was born, I was feeling distant from Les. Then I met this gorgeous dance teacher—his body, his face, everything was so beautiful. I was magnetized toward him. I would spend a long time doing my hair and having my clothes look right before going to his class. One day after class, I offered to give him a massage at my studio—it was the most sensual massage I've ever given. If he had made an advance toward me, I probably would have gone to bed with him, I wanted to jump him so bad. I was completely mesmerized. There was something about being seen by him."

"How did you handle it in your relationship?" I asked.

"I was up front with Les and said, 'Les, I'm not planning to leave you, but this guy is flipping me out. I haven't felt this way in a long, long time.' Les was freaked out, but he let me go through it. I just kept talking about it. He was so good, and didn't put me down even though he was upset. I'm glad to say we worked through it. What I've learned is that our relationship is so much about me being receptive. It's not about Les; he is romantic and he loves me. It's about me learning to open up. The amazing thing was that a year later, when the dance teacher came through town, I was pregnant, and I saw nothing in him."

Lily and Les both maintained their integrity during this difficult time. Lily was open about her attraction and her struggle, and Les, for the most part, did not take it as a negative reflection on himself. He could see it as something she was going through, and while it was very painful, he remained connected and didn't attack her.

For others, the line slips and there is an affair. When I work with couples struggling with a recent affair—or a recently revealed affair—I spend little time on the factual details other than how long, how many, what form it took, and help the couple explore the meaning of the affair. What was the status of the relationship before the affair? What did it mean to the person having the affair? Was the partner complicit with the affair in any way? What is the commitment to healing the relationship? What will it take to reinstate trust? I also explore the surrounding issues of alcohol, drugs, compulsive sexual behavior, and other addictions.

People have affairs for different reasons. In general, men have affairs to have sex, feel virile, excited, and attractive. Women have affairs because they feel they are dying in a relationship—they feel lonely, unhappy, and unappreciated. When someone shows romantic interest, it arouses those long-forgotten feelings of delight, anticipation, and sexual energy. It feels like coming alive. In other cases of repeated affairs, there is often a long history of sexually compulsive behavior that needs to be approached as an addiction.

Men and women both feel devastated by their partner's having an affair, but men often have a harder time letting go and taking responsibility for contributing to the decline of the relationship. Their ego is wounded and they are more prone to jab their partner with hostile reminders for years to come. Women compare themselves to the "other woman" and think that because he was sexual with her, he truly loved her. Most often, women want to maintain their relationship and, as a result, they are often more willing to forgive and focus on improving the relationship.

Shanda had an affair early in her tumultuous marriage with Mike. Mike was outraged, upset, and hurt. But he didn't want to leave the marriage. When they came for counseling four years after the affair, it was still an open wound for Mike, and Shanda was sick of hearing about it.

"How can we get past this?" Shanda asked.

"I think that's a question to ask Mike," I responded.

Mike's difficulty in letting go of the affair, even though Shanda was truly sorry and had been loyal ever since, turned out to be grounded in unresolved rage at his mother, along with a penetrating feeling of worthlessness. The affair gave him permission to feel righteous and angry—he had the goods on her. It took some time for him to realize that hanging on to his hurt and anger reinforced his sense of worthlessness, and, in a way, he was rubbing salt in his own wound.

In Buddhist terms, we could say he kept telling the story over and over, increasing his identity as a wounded victim. He needed to give up the power of bringing up the affair when he was angry. Shanda needed to let go of her guilt and set limits. She learned to say, "It's no fair bringing that up, let's talk about what's really going on right now."

Opening up to the feelings brought about by the affair allowed them to talk about their relationship and Mike's secret use of pornography—a contentious issue in their marriage. As Shanda gave up her guilt and Mike was able to explore the feelings of worthlessness he had tied to the affair, they eventually were able to put it to rest. He was able to see that she didn't do it to him so much as she did it to herself—she broke her vow and compromised her integrity. While it was an arduous process, their honest efforts together and willingness to be vulnerable allowed them to maintain their marriage, which recently hit the twenty-year mark.

If your eye is wandering and you feel enticed to cross that line, it's time to have an openhearted discussion with your partner about all aspects of your marriage. Affairs are hard to get over and usually leave a scar.

Our task in relationships is to make a conscious effort to stay connected with each other and to explore our sexuality as an integral part of that connection. Buddhism teaches that we are all made of the same energy. Our sexual relationship reflects the whole of who we are, merging with the whole of another person. A loving sexual bond, in which we dissolve into each other, allows us to experience the nature of unity and the melting of separateness.

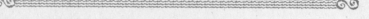

56 MAKE LOVE WITH A BEGINNER'S MIND

Is this then a touch? . . . quivering me
*   to a new identity,*
Flames and ether making a rush for my veins . . .
My flesh and blood playing out lightning,
to strike what is hardly different from myself
*   —Walt Whitman, LEAVES OF GRASS*

When you make love with a beginner's mind, you let your love spill out of you as your intuitive, creative side awakens. You absorb the wonder of creation happening in your moment-to-moment experience. You let your touch vibrate through you and into your beloved.

With a beginner's mind, we make love to our beloved for the

first time, because there is no past, no future, and no expectations. We are here with our lover to know each other, to feel the pleasure and wonder of these amazing bodies.

Imagine making love with a completely empty mind, and no memory of the past, only a ripe feeling of your love for your partner. Let your thoughts be only a wish that you both be happy, and feel love, and the source of all love.

Imagine, slowly, while looking at each other, gently touching or stroking one single place on the face—or wherever you feel drawn. Tune in completely to the sensations flowing through you. Be aware of your fingers connecting with your partner. In your heart, wish your beloved complete happiness. Tune in deeper and deeper, noticing how the sensations change, as if you were experiencing touch for the first time. Keep bringing your eyes back to each other. Be aware of the sensations of where your partner is touching you.

When you are ready, move your fingers just a little bit more, staying completely aware of your sensations. Go slowly, gently stroking your partner's face while connecting through your eyes. You might stay in one area for a long time or feel a desire to move. Never go faster than you can be totally attuned to each other. Explore. Notice any ripple of response from your partner or inside you. Allow your body and heart to take over, guiding your hand. Follow the subtle cues from each other, remembering there is no goal, no moment other than this.

As your touch moves from the face to the rest of the body, feel any awakening of energy and pleasure inside you. Let it come of its own. Remember to breathe and soften your belly. Take a long time. There is no goal, no plan. Only the touch of this moment, and this moment. Allow yourself to bask in it.

You may want to take turns in being the giver or the receiver.

If you do, allow yourself to be fully one or the other. As you start to kiss, feel all the sensations that arise as you intermingle your essence and bodies with each other. Go slowly. Savor the experience. Keep touching, kissing, stroking, as if you are exploring your beloved's body for the first time, as if this is the most amazing experience you've ever had.

Feel the softness and strength in your bodies. Touch in many ways—softly with the tips of your fingers, or pressing deeply—exploring, attuning to skin, muscles, bones, and emotions. Let the power of the energy that arises fill your body and expand, like a wave washing through you, like fire and thunder or the softness of a spring rain. Be completely in your body and let it do what it wants to do. If you start to hold back or thoughts interrupt your presence, breathe, soften your belly, and come back to the sensations of the moment. Ask for what you want. Look your partner in the eyes, and in the midst of the physical sensations be fused with a vibrant stillness that allows you to truly experience one another fully. Let the flames and ether come into your veins. Let your loving become a flow of giving and receiving that brings you pleasure and joy and then stillness.

Soft, powerful, sweet, joyful, natural.

PART NINE

I AND THOU: EVEN GOOD RELATIONSHIPS CAN GET BETTER

57 KEEP YOUR RELATIONSHIP DANCING

Exertion has a journey quality, a process quality . . .
How do we connect with inspiration? How do we
connect with the spark and joy that's available in
every moment?

—Pema Chodron

Just as the spiritual journey invites individuals to stay open to inspiration, creativity, and joy, the same applies to couples. Sometimes, it seems that life offers us enough challenges and we don't need to look for more, but other times, we get settled in our ways and the dance gets stale. Buddhism frequently speaks of the need to pull the rug out from under ourselves to avoid complacency, so that we maintain an open hand to life without grasping or clinging. Otherwise, we're just shuffling around.

The concept of exertion, one of the six paramitas—or instructions on wholesome behavior—means going beyond resistance or complacency to find something more expansive and wonderful on the other side. For me, it often takes the form of practicing the piano instead of watching TV, of taking a brisk morning walk up Blue Mountain to hear the meadowlarks instead of sleeping longer. It takes effort at first, but I'm much happier as a result.

As applied to relationships, exertion could mean initiating a conversation with your partner about a difficult subject you've been avoiding. While it's scary, it has the potential to lead to greater understanding and kindness between you. Exertion could also take the form of bringing your partner flowers, arranging a surprise date, or writing a love poem. It could also relate to moving, having children, not having children, starting a project, letting go of material possessions, or going for counseling. Exertion helps keep a relationship in motion—learning new steps, dancing and moving to new songs.

If you want to bring more vitality into your union, take time with your partner to talk about the things you enjoy doing together as a couple, and then go even further to discuss any new interests you'd like to explore together. Then make plans.

The more you bond together in present time, the more you will deepen your sense of connection. To experiment with this idea, if you are taking a walk, talk only about what you are seeing or feeling in the moment—Oh look, see the eagle. My hiking friend Sue and I sometimes stop on the trail and stand still for a long time, listening deeper and deeper to the songs of the birds, the nearby stream, and the wind in the pines. The longer we stay there the more layers of sounds emerge. It's a form of ecstatic union with each other embraced by the vastness and wonder of nature. It allows us to connect in that place beyond words. Spend time together without discussing other people, injustice, politics, or *how bad it is* in the world. Leave all negativity behind. Be completely in the present, whether you are trying out a new recipe, planting a garden, or doing a project. If your mind wanders off take a breath, go inside, and come back to the present—the only place where love exists.

Sometimes, it helps to remember what you did when you were courting or first becoming involved with each other. Remember those walks, kissing and hugging on the couch, leisurely dinners? Mutual enjoyment can be simple—browsing in a bookstore together and having coffee, taking a walk, inviting some friends for a simple potluck, going to a sporting event, bicycling, taking an afternoon drive, doing a household project, planning a weekend getaway. Make a list of all the things that come to each of you that you would enjoy doing. Find the things you already know you like to do, then talk about fantasies and other interests. Bring something new into your lives. It will feed the spirit of your union.

John Gottman found in his research that successful relationships "come down to one simple mathematical formula: no matter what style your marriage follows, you must have at least five times as many positive as negative moments together if your marriage is to be stable."

This encouragement to have pleasure together may appear in contradiction with Buddhism, which stresses service to others as crucial to the spiritual path. Loving service is the ultimate measure of a good life, but it must come from a wellspring of life, and not from some nagging sense of duty or chronic guilt and worry about others. So many people are mired down in unhappy relationships, demanding jobs, or caring for children, or routinely feel guilt-ridden into meeting the wants of others while ignoring their own. Mutual pleasure and spending time together bring us closer to our hearts, help us feel delight, are good for our health, and help our relationship flourish.

Sometimes, keeping a relationship alive requires a major change in lifestyle. Several of my friends decided that they didn't want the stress and pressure of two full-time working parents with small children, so one became the home parent for a few years and they lived very simply. This enabled them to have more time together. Marie and Lawrence uprooted themselves from a successful career as musicians in San Diego to move to a pleasant college town that better suited the lifestyle they wanted for themselves and their children. It was a big risk, without much certainty of work, but they approached it as an adventure and are now living the lifestyle they want.

Still, it's important to remember that there is no one way to keep a relationship alive. What's important is for both people to take time to explore what feeds them as a couple, break through any resistance, and take action. If you are living with regrets or hopes that something will change in the future, you are creating duality inside. Remember: There is only now, there is only this moment, this day, this week. Don't put off doing what feeds the hand of life. This is a very special moment. All of them are.

58 BE CREATIVE TOGETHER

It is not necessary to have great things to do
I turn my little omelet in the pan for the love of God
—Brother Lawrence

Every stroke of my brush
Is the overflow
Of my inmost heart
—Sengai

If creative endeavors are the overflow of one's inmost heart, then when we join our beloved in a creative venture, we are truly bringing our hearts together . . . along with the muses and the mystery of creation. Creativity flourishes when we are completely in the present moment and allow our inner world to unfold. Whether it's cooking an omelette, designing a garden, moving the furniture around, or planning a vacation, we can allow our creativity to bring us together. When we set aside our egos and take on a project together, we enter into a process of creating something together that grows from the best of both of us. If it's an actual project—adding a porch, starting a garden, decorating a living room—we brainstorm all the possibilities or keep our mind on the shared goal. We build on each other's ideas. The conversation might include phrases such as: "Here's an idea." "What if we did this?" "Well, maybe if we combined these two ideas." It is the push and pull of ideas erupting and building on each other that help us to create something better than either of us could have done alone.

If you can join together in the "us" place, knowing that being creative together is more important than anyone being right or winning, you can add spark to your relationship. It doesn't matter if every leaf is raked perfectly, or if the dessert is a flop, or whether or not the new rosebush eventually looks like the picture on the package—it's that the two of you joined in stretching, exploring, and joining together to bring new life to the ordinary tasks of everyday living.

Creativity is like the breath of spirit circulating freely within us, blowing out tired assumptions and perceptions of how things should be, and taking us back to beginner's mind, that childlike state that, free from rules, resonates with possibilities and delight.

59 REMEMBER, OUR TASK IS TO EXPAND OUR LOVE— NOT TO CHANGE OTHERS

The journey takes place inside each of us—seeing the flowers, the weeds, the cobwebs, the shadows. The journey is not about instructing our partner to look at their own weeds and shadows, although our relationship is likely to bring these things to the surface.

At the heart of the spiritual journey, we allow ourselves to be at one with this living, breathing moment. Instead of creating scripts and pictures of how we want things to be, we step into each moment with complete awareness, and then respond from what arises within us, tempered by respect and good wishes. So if our partner blames us or yells at us, we can respond, "I don't like to be yelled at," but we don't need to turn it into deep psychological inquiry. We can remind ourselves that when someone is being cruel or unkind, it stems from his or her internal suffering or ignorance. We can set limits and respond simply, without throwing the other person out of our heart.

When we try to mold our partner into an idealized picture of what we want, we are getting caught up in attachments: I am attached to you being sweeter, more talkative, and so on. It's as if we're really saying, "I can't love you as you are, so please change to fit my narrow picture of what I can love." It is especially damaging when we try to change our partner's character or personality. I'm not referring to direct requests like "I don't like it when you clutter up the living room." That's clear and straightforward.

It's about covert and overt ways in which we attempt to manipulate or change our partner because we can't accept him for who he is.

When relationships become our spiritual journey, we see our beloved just as she is—foibles, flaws, and wondrous traits. This doesn't mean we have to like everything, it just means that we live in reality. We see the package with all its parts, not just the sweet, romantic part we like best. What I repeatedly see with couples is someone hoping her partner will always be like his best, sexiest part. I ask her to draw a circle and write all her partner's traits in the circle. That's the reality—the package deal. She will argue, "But I think this sweet, kind part is his *real* self. Don't you think if he worked on it, he could always be like that?"

"That's not the issue." I reply. "All we can go on is today, and how your partner is right now. The problem is not with him, it's about your images and attachments." Can you look at a package as a whole and know it's all part of who he is? Can you stretch yourself to love more fully right now?

Marie and Lawrence talked about the tempestuous time of their early relationship before one of their several separations, when they split with the intention of never seeing each other again. "I had this picture of the man I wanted to be with," Marie said. "Lawrence wasn't it. He was short, balding, and ordinary-looking. He wasn't flashy, seductive, or charming . . . like some of these horrible men I kept seeing," she added with a laugh. "We fought about nearly everything, because I wanted him to be something he wasn't, and he kept rebelling against me. It was years later, when he moved in as a housemate with me and my daughter, that I started to see him as Lawrence, this man who was tender and loving with my child, this kind person who was reliable and steadfast in his care for me. This person who was such a good friend. There was so much we loved to do together—biking, hiking, making music. As I let go of trying to change him, the old picture started to melt and we stopped fighting so much. I had to ask myself, what was my picture about anyhow? Some of the men who had fit the handsome, charming image had been selfish and mean to me—sexy but empty."

Lawrence added, "In those early days, I felt rebellious all the time. It was as if nothing I did was right, like someone chipping away at who I was. It hurt and left me feeling just like I did as a child—the odd one out who was never good enough. That's when I left for a year—I even left the country to get as far away as I could."

As each of them gained awareness of themselves and reflected inward, the dynamics changed. Marie stopped trying to change Lawrence, and he learned to stand up for himself. She became more in alignment with the task of lovingkindness, which allowed her to see beneath the surface into the heart of her beloved—this tender, struggling soul, wanting love, meaning, and purpose in life, the same as we all do. She went from I-object, to I-thou. She could see Lawrence for who he was, not through the filter of an image she had created.

Jill talked about a time in her marriage when her husband repeatedly made sideways remarks about her body—your belly is so round, your thighs have changed, and so on. She felt wounded and depressed as she allowed his comments to penetrate her. He had crossed a line by criticizing her body instead of looking at his difficulty being sexually aroused. She had colluded by feeling ashamed. Then, one day a flash of anger surged through her. She threw off her bathrobe and stood before him naked. "This is the body I live in," she said. "This is how it is. It's a good body, it's me, it's sexy, it's the person you married, and I never want to hear any more comments or criticism." That was the end of it.

Her powerful stance brought both of them into reality of the present moment, and, as a result, they both expanded and came closer. He let go of his unrealistic image of the female form and met her as she was, and she stopped feeling ashamed of her body and stopped allowing his image to dictate her feelings about herself. They became a grown-up man and woman together.

Buddhism uses the image of washing the dirt off the windows so you can see clearly, without the veils of your illusions. That is the task of love—to see your partner clearly, to let go of your images and enter the dance of relationship with this flesh-and-blood, perfectly imperfect being you have chosen as your beloved. It's to journey side by side, both becoming more of who you really are, enjoying the drama and the dance. Only then do we enter the shared heart of the beloved, where we can drop our ego boundaries and experience a deep and abiding love for each other.

60 ACCEPT LIFE'S DAILY LOSSES

The clouds pass and the rain does its work,
and all individual beings flow into their forms
—I CHING

An undercurrent of sadness is inherent to life. We are continuously dying into life, dying into the moment. To be in the flow of the present moment, we must let go of yesterday, of five minutes ago—the touch, the conversation, the togetherness, the hurt, the argument, the lingering kiss. If we try to capture a moment, we are not living it. If we try to re-create it, we are pining away for the past. This is now, this is all we have. This moment just passed, now another moment, another thought, another tear, a feeling of happiness, sadness. Just like the breath we just exhaled—it will never be the same.

Likewise, in relationships, what once brought pleasure often fades, sometimes for only one partner.

Marge and Betty routinely got up Sunday morning, bought the *New York Times*, played recordings of classical music, made special coffee, scrambled eggs, and hung out together reading and chatting. Then, one Saturday evening, Betty said she was planning to attend a religious meeting the next morning. Something was missing for her and she wanted to find a spiritual community that fit for her.

Marge initially felt a pang of hurt. The ritual she treasured would be interrupted, possibly gone forever. She allowed herself to feel the loss, and in doing so could express both her sadness and her support for Betty taking a new step in her life. The next morning, when she was alone at home on a Sunday morning for the first time in over a year, her initial emptiness gave way to writing letters to some old friends. Afterward, she took a walk, and started reflecting on the status of her own life. While she didn't like the change, she allowed the emptiness to be a doorway to something new evolving for her.

If Marge was unwilling to feel the loss, the conversation might have gone like this.

Marge: "But we always spend Sunday morning together."

Betty: "I know, but I feel drawn to visit the Quaker meeting."

"Is it more important than me?"

"No, please understand, it's not about you, it's about something I need."

"Why do you need it?" Marge says, her voice rising.

"I don't know, really, I just want to go."

"You don't even know why you're going, and you're ruining our time together. Don't I matter to you?"

Then Betty starts feeling guilty, angry, and frustrated. "Yes, you matter, but I wish you could think of me for a change. Why is everything about what you want?"

And on and on. If we believe a ritual—such as Sunday-morning brunch—defines our relationship and is a measure of our connection, we see the loss of it as loss of the relationship, as opposed to a time of change. To stay on the path we need to allow the loss to be felt. When we create images of what brought pleasure and try to re-create them, we are likely to be disappointed. The summer cabin that felt so romantic may or may not hold the same enchantment when we visit it five years later.

We seek comfort, security, and reliable rituals as a shield against the inevitable losses that create a stream of melancholy that flows through life. I have this predictable relationship, this marriage, this home, this great sex life, and I want to keep it this way. We also confine ourselves when we seek security with schedules, food, clothes, TV, exercise routines, even with meditation and spiritual practice. There is nothing wrong with a schedule, but when we get attached to it and can't accept change, we get stuck. If we are uneasy all day because we didn't have our morning run, make love, meditate, drink orange juice, or read the paper, then we've become attached to our ritual. We need to let go.

To feel free, we need to remember that all things pass away, and we will too. One of us will probably die before the other, and one of us will be left alone. If we live with an open hand, never grabbing hold of images or moments, we will accept the pangs of loss that inevitably come with change.

Don't let the ground under your feet get too solid. Don't get too secure or caught in your ways, because it puts you to sleep, and from that sleep state a loss can feel jarring or even cata-strophic, instead of natural. True stability is rooted in a love that lives within us, a love that flows through all our relationships.

When love is ripe and rich within us, we have a safe harbor inside no matter what dramas are unfolding around us, no matter if our house burns down or we lose a job. From this place, loss is experi-enced as something passing through us, but not of great importance.

I spoke with Ruth about losses in relationships.

"We help each other get a perspective when there is a sudden loss," she said. "If the car gets banged up, or we lose twenty thou-sand dollars in a business, or one of our children is unhappy, we help each other remember what's important in life—that we're alive, we have love, we have each other. Alone, we might get de-pressed over these losses, but together we bring each other back to reality. Neither of us puts a lot of importance in material objects."

To face the little daily losses is like practice for the big losses, including death. It all becomes part of the flow of life. We grieve a loss but we also move on. A dear friend of mine who lost his beloved wife to cancer went through a period of deep sorrow, but two years later, he was remarried and feeling great joy in life.

Recently, at a backyard reception following a memorial service for my favorite aunt, Janet, there was an array of life's special mo-ments being celebrated. Janet's daughter Emily brought out a box of old photos for us to go through and take from. One couple announced they were pregnant, another talked about their im-pending marriage, and a large birthday cake was brought out to celebrate three birthdays in the coming week. It felt like a feast of life wound together.

The deepest practice for accepting loss is to remember that we are all part of the flow of consciousness. We come into this earth in a physical body and we will leave this body behind, and go back to the sea of All That Is—the universal mind or consciousness. We remember that while our minds, emotions, and lives pass through us, they are ephemeral, they are not who we are.

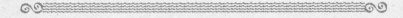

61 RELATIONSHIPS NEED TENDING, AND TENDING TAKES TIME

It should seem obvious that an emotional investment in a relationship takes time, but this concept seems to elude many people. We harbor some vague myth that relationships just happen. But that's completely wrong. If we have a fairly good relationship and do nothing to keep it alive, it will slide downhill. We need to invest time and energy in each other for our relationship to flourish.

People who keep relationships alive make dates with each other, take time to talk, make love, and have fun. They find a way to spend private time away from their children. In other words, they make their relationship a high priority. Even if they work long hours or have lots of stress in their lives, the relationship is center stage and it's given attention. When a couple is well bonded and united in the "us" place, then parenting, work, and relationships with others are all enhanced. Too often, people substitute children, work, or some hobby or sport for what is missing in the relationship.

If we want houseplants to stay alive, we water them. If we want them to thrive, we find the place that gives them the best amount of light, we pick off dead leaves, we notice if the soil is too dry or too damp. As the sun shifts its light throughout the seasons, we might try different locations, especially if the plant isn't doing well—maybe more light, maybe less. If this is what it takes to have a healthy plant, then ponder the need to tend a relationship.

While having pleasure with each other is not just about the number of hours spent together, in general, loving couples make time together a priority. Of course, there will be times in a marriage when one person is less available due to work, illness, caring for a parent, or other concerns. But sometimes we get so busy we don't notice that we are rarely with our partner. To explore this, add up the hours in your week you spend at work, and sleeping. Then think of all the other hours. How much time do you spend separate from your partner? How much time do you spend with your partner?

If you are not making time to be together, ask yourself: Is it because you have become inattentive to the relationship and need to reaffirm your commitment? Or is it because times together have become empty, contentious, or dull? If it's the latter, then it's time for a heart-to-heart exploration of what's troubling both of you. And, remember, if a gulf has grown between you, it won't get better by doing nothing. The unattended flower wilts. There is no time like now to open up. The time and effort it takes to sit down and talk may be scary, but what you really should fear is alienation, loneliness, loss of connection, and the resulting poverty of life that comes from holding back and keeping distance. Ultimately, it's not just about how much time we spend together, it's having moments when we truly take delight in each other's company.

62 YOUR LOVING RELATIONSHIP BLESSES THE WORLD

> *Love, which is the very energy and expression of life,*
> *   is whole.*
> *Thought cannot approach this energy. Words can-*
> *   not capture it*
> *It is us all, and all of us. This is not the answer to*
> *   our question*
> *It is the question fallen silent.*
> — Steven Harrison,
> GETTING TO WHERE YOU ARE

Eastern traditions use the phrase "*neti, neti*" in many spiritual teachings—it means "not that, not that." When we seek to understand love, we might first ask what love is not. Love is not emotion, not attraction, not sentiment, not sensation, not attachment, not possession, not dependency, not need; it is not using someone to fill an emptiness, to make us feel important, or to shore up our ego. No words can capture love because it is eternal, beyond thought.

Love awaits us beneath our anger, fear, sorrow, and hopelessness. Love is a process that evolves over time, through shared experiences of giving, receiving, knowing, change, and loss. We learn to stay clear with each other through a profound level of honesty. We comfort and cherish each other. We laugh, cry, and play together.

Love happens naturally when the mind and heart are free of

fear—when there is no protection, no holding back. Fear dissolves as we come together without effort, without trying, without worry, without an agenda. We join in the river of life together and let the water carry us.

When we live in the heart of love, our daily experience becomes one of awe and wonder at everything from a new leaf on a plant, to the smile of a friend, to noticing the weaving together of threads in a cloth. Our thoughts and emotions rise and fall as we remain connected to a deeper unifying force that binds us all together.

As partners and friends, our love becomes a mirror that reflects our potential and strengths that we carry with us into the world. We become both the candle and the flame. We join a circle where giving and receiving melt into a single energy as we become genuine and generous, wanting the absolute best for all people. It is not surprising that all of the successful couples I interviewed were engaged in community service in myriad ways.

Recently, there was an article in the local paper about the death of Maureen Mansfield, who was married to Mike Mansfield, a beloved five-term senator from Montana. "The real credit for whatever standing I have in life should be given to my wife, Maureen," Mike Mansfield said. "She was and is my inspiration." Inseparable for sixty-eight years of marriage, and always a team, they met in Butte, Montana, where she was teaching high school English and Mike was working in the local copper mine. In his words, "She encouraged and literally forced a dropout eighth-grader to achieve a university degree and at the same time make up his high school credits. She sold her life insurance and gave up her job as a teacher to make it possible. . . . She has always been the better half of our lives together. . . . In short, I am what I am because of her."

But this is not a story of a woman sacrificing her life for her partner. It is a story of two people who brought out the absolute best in each other. She radiated warmth and kindness, supported many humanitarian programs, and lived the life she wanted. A friend commented, "I don't think anybody will ever know how much she influenced his decisions, but I think it was tremendous. What a partnership! They are two kind, decent people who made their lives what they were by trying to make something better for everyone."

Our relationships are embedded in community. The world lives in us and we live in the world. It's a wheel within a wheel—an endless circle of ever-changing connections. Our home base of a loving relationship helps us reach out to others, to radiate a healing energy to our friends and loved ones. Ultimately, love is not something we seek; rather, it lives in us, between us, and around us. Manifest in the world, we become part of something vast and intangible as we come into a felt relationship with everyone. As we tap deeper and deeper into that wellspring of love that rests at the center of all of us, we become the message and the messenger.

With peace and gratitude,
Your sister,
CHARLOTTE SOPHIA

RECOMMENDED READING

Instead of an extensive bibliography, I have listed some of my favorite books on relationships and spirituality.

RELATIONSHIPS

Chopra, Deepak. *The Path to Love: Spiritual Strategies for Healing.*
Fromm, Erich. *The Art of Loving.*
Johnson, Catherine. *Lucky in Love.*
Johnson, Susan. *Staying Power: Long Term Lesbian Couples.*
Kasl, Charlotte, *Finding Joy.*
————. *A Home for the Heart: Creating Intimacy and Community with Loved Ones, Neighbors, and Friends.*
————. *Women, Sex, and Addicton: A Search for Love and Power.*
Levine, Stephen, and Ondrea Levine. *Embracing the Beloved.*
Luhrs, Janet. *Simple Loving.*
Pearsall, Paul. *Sexual Healing.*
Scarf, Maggie. *Intimate Partners: Patterns in Love and Marriage.*
Schaeffer, Brenda. *Is It Love or Is It Addiction?*
————. *Love's Way.*

BUDDHISM AND RELATED TOPICS

Boorstein, Sylvia. *It's Easier Than You Think*, and other titles.

Chodron, Pema. *Start Where You Are: A Guide to Compassionate Living.*

———. *When Things Fall Apart: Heart Advice for Difficult Times.*

———. *The Wisdom of No Escape: And the Path of Loving-Kindness*

Das, Lama Surya. *Awakening the Buddha Within.*

Epstein, Mark, M.D. *Thoughts Without a Thinker.*

Kasl, Charlotte, *If the Buddha Dated.*

Linssen, Robert. *Living Zen.*

Nhat Hanh, Thich. *The Diamond That Cuts Through Illusion.*

———. *The Heart of Understanding: Commentaries on the Prajna-paramita Heart Sutra.*

———. *Peace Is Every Step: The Path of Mindfulness in Everyday Life.*

Pauling, Chris. *Introducing Buddhism.*

Rahula, Walpola. *What the Buddha Taught.*

Salzberg, Sharon. *Lovingkindness: The Revolutionary Art of Happiness.*

Suzuki, Shunryu. *Zen Mind, Beginner's Mind.*

SPIRITUALITY

Gibran, Kahlil. *The Prophet.*

Harrison, Steven. *Getting to Where You Are.*

Krishnamurti, J. *The Book of Life.*

———. *The First and the Last Freedom.*

———. *On Fear.*

———. *On Relationship.*

Maharaj, Sri Nisargadatta. *I Am That.*

————. *Seeds of Consciousness*.
Nadeen, Satyam. *From Onions to Pearls*.
Tolle, Eckhart. *The Power of Now*.

POETRY

Barks, Coleman, and John Moyne, translator. *The Essential Rumi*.
————. *Like That*.
————. *Say I Am You: Poetry Interspersed with Stories of Rumi and Shams*.
Bly, Robert. *The Kabir Book: Forty-four of the Ecstatic Poems of Kabir*.
Whitman, Walt. *Leaves of Grass*.

PSYCHOLOGY

Miller, Jean Baker, M.D. *Toward a New Psychology of Women*.
Watkins, John, and Helen Watkins. *Ego State Therapy*.
Wolinsky, Stephen. *The Dark Side of the Inner Child*.
————. *Intimate Relationships: Why the Do and Do Not Work*.
————. *Quantum Consciousness*.
————. *The Tao of Chaos*.
————. *Trances People Live*.
————. *The Way of the Human*.

GENERAL READING

Havel, Vaclav. *Living in Truth*.
————. *Summer Meditations*.
Rosenberg, Marshall, Ph.D. *Nonviolent Communication*.

RESOURCES

MARATHON PSYCHOTHERAPY

I (Charlotte Kasl) am available for marathon psychotherapy sessions for individuals and couples. I use a combination of EMDR, ego-state therapy, hypnosis, quantum psychology, and body movement. I am a licensed clinical counselor in Montana, and a certified addiction specialist. Call (406) 273-6080 for information.

EMDR (EYE MOVEMENT DESENSITIZATION AND REPROCESSING)

This is an advanced technology that accesses the brain and helps release traumatic memories, change behavior patterns, and overcome addictive and compulsive behavior. It is very focused, efficient, and effective. For more information, you can read *EMDR* by Francine Shapiro (HarperCollins), or look on the Internet. For a therapist in your area, or for information, write or call EMDR, P.O. Box 51010, Pacific Grove, CA 93950, (831) 372-3900; fax: (831) 647-9881.

CORRESPONDENCE

I love to receive letters and read them all, but I can't promise to respond. If you want to be on a mailing list or receive information on workshops, enclose a self-addressed, stamped, legal-sized envelope. I do not have referrals for therapists.

I am available for workshops, talks, consulting, and therapist trainings on a variety of topics related to dating, relationships, sexuality, finding joy, addiction, spirituality, and empowerment.

Charlotte Kasl, Ph.D
P.O. Box 1302
Lolo, MT 59847
(406) 273-6080; fax: (406) 273-0111

FOR THE BEST IN PAPERBACKS, LOOK FOR THE

In every corner of the world, on every subject under the sun, Penguin represents quality and variety—the very best in publishing today.

For complete information about books available from Penguin—including Puffins, Penguin Classics, and Compass—and how to order them, write to us at the appropriate address below. Please note that for copyright reasons the selection of books varies from country to country.

In the United Kingdom: Please write to *Dept. EP, Penguin Books Ltd, Bath Road, Harmondsworth, West Drayton, Middlesex UB7 0DA.*

In the United States: Please write to *Penguin Putnam Inc., P.O. Box 12289 Dept. B, Newark, New Jersey 07101-5289* or call 1-800-788-6262.

In Canada: Please write to *Penguin Books Canada Ltd, 10 Alcorn Avenue, Suite 300, Toronto, Ontario M4V 3B2.*

In Australia: Please write to *Penguin Books Australia Ltd, P.O. Box 257, Ringwood, Victoria 3134.*

In New Zealand: Please write to *Penguin Books (NZ) Ltd, Private Bag 102902, North Shore Mail Centre, Auckland 10.*

In India: Please write to *Penguin Books India Pvt Ltd, 11 Panchsheel Shopping Centre, Panchsheel Park, New Delhi 110 017.*

In the Netherlands: Please write to *Penguin Books Netherlands bv, Postbus 3507, NL-1001 AH Amsterdam.*

In Germany: Please write to *Penguin Books Deutschland GmbH, Metzlerstrasse 26, 60594 Frankfurt am Main.*

In Spain: Please write to *Penguin Books S. A., Bravo Murillo 19, 1° B, 28015 Madrid.*

In Italy: Please write to *Penguin Italia s.r.l., Via Benedetto Croce 2, 20094 Corsico, Milano.*

In France: Please write to *Penguin France, Le Carré Wilson, 62 rue Benjamin Baillaud, 31500 Toulouse.*

In Japan: Please write to *Penguin Books Japan Ltd, Kaneko Building, 2-3-25 Koraku, Bunkyo-Ku, Tokyo 112.*

In South Africa: Please write to *Penguin Books South Africa (Pty) Ltd, Private Bag X14, Parkview, 2122 Johannesburg.*